CHARMS, SPELLS, AND CURSES
FOR THE MILLIONS

CHARMS, SPELLS, AND CURSES FOR THE MILLIONS

by

V. J. Banis

Writing as "Victor Samuels"

The Borgo Press
An Imprint of Wildside Press
MMVII

FIRST WILDSIDE EDITION

Contents

Introduction

In this country and time, magic is very much in disrepute. Bring the subject up at a dinner gathering, and most of those present, if not all, will wrinkle their noses in amusement and openly pooh-pooh the matter. But what is truly amusing is that these same skeptics remain unaware of how strong and ingrained is their belief in the supernatural and how often they appeal to it.

"Of course I don't believe in magic. Oh, good luck on your trip." "There's no such thing; I make my own luck, and I plan to continue doing so, knock on wood." "People are finally coming to realize how silly all this supernatural nonsense is, Lord willing." Such conversational paradoxes would be funny if they weren't so common and so unconscious.

The truth is, we all believe in magic to some extent and try to influence natural events by its use, whether we cross our fingers, knock on wood, avoid black cats, hesitate to walk under ladders, blow out a match before the third cigarette is lit, toss spilled salt over our left shoulders, wish one another luck, wear good luck charms, carry rabbit's feet, finger rosaries, pray, become nervous on Friday the thirteenth, or perform any of hundreds of symbolic gestures that have carried down to us from generations of believers.

If we are reluctantly persuaded to admit that we do use certain magic charms and conjurations, we are often downright horrified that anyone should think we actually believe in them, or expect them to work, or give any credence to witches.

Here again, we make liars and fools of ourselves. It would be sheer nonsense to say that witches haven't existed and don't exist right now. And they use magic, in many instances the same sort of magic we all utilize. And the simple truth is, it works—at least, some of the time.

In some instances, there is absolutely nothing surprising about this success. Any man of science who examines the history of witchcraft, for instance, will discover that witches have always concentrated a great deal of their attention on healing physical ailments, frequently by the use of herbs. And a little examination will prove that some of their cures had every reason to work. Often the witches of the Middle Ages were expert herbalists, using healing techniques that have since become commonplace. It was once thought clever to laugh at the witches of England who used a type of mold to heal various ailments—until we discovered the healing powers of penicillin, which is produced from mold. Witch doctors amused Britishers with their use of a certain drug to heal "illnesses of the soul," until someone investigated this strange drug and found the parent of the modern-day tranquilizer. Witches recommended frog's eggs as a sort of disinfectant; today we know that they have a high iodine content. Many witch recipes called for plantain leaves or roots. The late W. H. Box, a world-famous authority on herbalism, has said that plantain could cure almost anything, from poisoning to piles.

The power of suggestion was no doubt a powerful factor working in the witch's favor, especially through the centuries in which people's faith was strong—faith in God, in Satan, and in hosts of other forces.

As to whether there was something more involved than fundamental scientific luck and the power of suggestion—well, nothing will be accomplished by reopening that quarrel. Our purpose here has been to bring together a collection of specific charms, curses, and spells in a sort of "recipe book" or "how-to." There are plenty of other volumes on the subjects of witchcraft and magic, but all too often they deal in vague generalities or mumbo jumbo and tell us *about* this or the other spell but never get around to telling us the spell itself. We have avoided that here, within certain limitations —obviously some of the ingredients may sound strange to the modern reader. If we were to try to provide encyclopedic information on every item mentioned, we would probably get through no more than half a dozen spells. We have, for instance, included certain spells from the Egyptian magical writings. But we could have devoted at least one volume, more probably several, to trying to explain the heirarchy of Egyptian gods and goddesses, the fine points of their beliefs, and other relevant facts. We have chosen instead to present the spells and charms themselves, as often as possible in their original forms or in the simplest translations. They come from a variety of sources—English, Scotch, Egyptian, Chaldean, Babylonian, American, French, Greek, Roman. Some are as old as man himself. Others are apparently modern. Some have the ring of fine verse; others have only the clumsiest literary style.

Likewise, while we have tried to categorize the spells for the reader's convenience, these categories have necessarily proven arbitrary time and again, and if a spell does not appear in the chapter in which it seems to belong, please read on; it may yet appear in some other section to which it seemed to us better suited.

A word of caution—no claims are made for the efficacy of any of these writings. They are presented as found and are offered as a matter of interest to students of the occult. If the novice should wish to try them and they should produce results, well, that is his good fortune. If they do not—well, we can only cross our fingers and try again.

CHAPTER ONE

Healing Methods

It was in the healing of disease that the witch or practioner of black magic came closest to being a specialist, and we cannot really afford to take their contributions lightly. Suggestions that men of science once thought laughable have proven to have bases in scientific fact—while much of what was once considered to be scientific fact is now laughable.

We tend to smile tolerantly when we learn that in many parts of the world people still turn to the local witch, witch doctor, or "peculiar old woman" for strange-sounding medical treatments. But if we are honest, we must admit there is not much difference between the primitive man who believes that the "juices of a turtle" will cure his physical aches and such modern children of science as the author himself, who adheres to a rather pleasant cold-cure, the sipping of hot toddies. Medical science refuses to

11

corroborate what the users know, that these brews do make one feel better.

We are all aware of the use of suggestion in medicine; we know that doctors may prescribe harmless sugar pills for some patients. Christian Scientists and others rely more or less exclusively upon what is in effect the power of suggestion. Everyone laughs when chicken soup is referred to as "Jewish penicillin"—but we have no reservations about taking this timeless medicine.

The healing methods of witches in the Middle Ages were, in fact, probably at least as effective as those of the doctors of the time—and quite possibly more so.

Lignite (a variety of coal), if bound on the forehead, stops bleeding of the nose and restores lost senses.

Diamond is an effective antidote against the pestilence.

Chelidonium (an herb), if put in a yellow linen cloth and tied about the neck, will certainly cure fever.

Heliotrope stops bleeding and averts any danger from poison.

The following incantation will cure a child of worms:

> Holy Monday
> Holy Tuesday
> Holy Wednesday
> Maundy Thursday

12

Good Friday
Holy Saturday
Easter Sunday
Worms on the run day.

Repeat this incantation backwards, then forward, then backwards over the child.

The skin disease erysipelas can be cured by the application of silver to the afflicted area.

The sapphire has an especial property in that it prevents the eye from being affected by smallpox.

Egg Limpia: A limpia is advised for illness of the soul. The best is the Egg Limpia. A likeness of the patient's face is drawn on an eggshell. The patient lies flat on the floor. The one conducting the limpia sucks away the evil by sucking certain regions such as the temples, the breast, the crook of the arm, until they redden considerably or until blood specks appear on the skin, indicating that the evil is beginning to emerge. When this soul poison has been brought to the surface, the egg is rolled all over the patient's body. In this manner the evil is tricked into leaving the body and going into the egg, which it mistakes for the patient. When the egg has had time to absorb all the traces of the evil, cleansing herbs are sprinkled lavishly over the patient. He should then use an inhaling limpia, which is prepared in the following manner: the beard is cut off a billy goat; tie this at one end, pass it over an open flame, and inhale the pungent smoke. Another inhaling limpia is done with laurel leaves steeped in water, and either of these will suffice. If the soul illness is minor, an inhaling limpia alone may suffice to cure the condition. When the patient has inhaled the fumes as prescribed, the doctor may breath all over the patient for purification, and the process will be more effective if prayers have been said constantly throughout. Here a chicken may be used as well; if so, it too is passed over the patient after the sucking. In either form, the egg is broken afterward. The egg matter is smeared over the patient's face and then washed off with water in which laurel leaves have been steeped. The full limpia is now done and the soul will be well again.

In case of illness, anoint or bathe the patient with rosemary water while praying over him. To make the water, steep two handfuls of rosemary leaves in two quarts of water overnight, having poured the water over the leaves while boiling.

Jacinth or hyacinth is a stone which strengthens the heart and is recommended as a soporific. It is ordered in cases of cough, rupture, and melancholy, in any of which cases it is to be drunk with vinegar.

Cagliostro's Rejuvenation Course, by which the true sage is able to renew his youth, not once but time and again: A forty-day preparation must be performed every fifteen years. The first full moon in the month of May is chosen for the start of the process, which has to be carried out in the company of only one companion, who must be dedicated. Only dew is drunk, and this must be collected from the shoots of germinating corn upon a cloth made of the purest linen. For food the sage might nibble upon a piece of bread or biscuit. On the seventeenth day of the course, some blood is let. From this date

14

after, Balm of Azoth is taken each morning and night. Six drops are to be taken on the eighteenth day; then the dose can be increased each day by two drops until the thirty-second day. On the dawn of the thirty-third day of the retreat a fresh bloodletting must be performed. Once this is done, the patient will immediately go to bed until the close of the fortieth day. As soon as the patient awakes after the second bleeding, he must take a grain of the Universal Medicine, which can be expected to produce convulsions, excessive perspiration, and purging in most cases. Now the subject may be permitted to take a little broth which has been made from lean meat, together with rice, valerian, vervain, and balm. The next day another grain of Universal Medicine will be taken. This medicine will be known as astral mercury in combination with sulphur of gold. On the thirty-sixth day a glass of Egyptian wine is drunk. On the following day the last grain of the Universal Medicine is taken. At this stage the patient may expect to fall into a deep sleep. During this sleep the hair, the teeth, the nails, and the skin will be renewed. On the thirty-eighth day a warm bath must be taken; herbs must be steeped in the water, and these will be rice, valerian, vervain, and balm. When the thirty-ninth day breaks, the patient must drink ten drops of Acharat Elixir in the medium of a small amount of red wine. On the fortieth day the subject will find that the work of rejuvenation has been completed and youth has been returned.

Jasper is a stone which prevents fever and dropsy. It is also highly reputed as a preservative against defluxions, the nightmare, and epilepsy.

Among the objects which possess curative properties are the bones of toads, old coins, and the teeth of wolves.

To cure most colds, take garlic cloves and chop them and wrap them in a small bundle. The patient must be put to bed under warm covers with the garlic bundle in a position as close as possible to his nose, to insure the constant breathing of the strong fumes.

Any medicine that contains gold leaf is especially effective in curing.

To cure drunkenness, ashes of toad mixed with brandy.

To ease the pain a baby suffers in teething, hang around its little neck a tooth extracted from a live mouse.

If the body is afflicted, take an eggshell and stuff it with horsehair; rub this on the afflicted part and it will absorb the disease, after which the eggshell and the disease may be easily discarded.

Betony, any plant of the figwort tree, gives relief from toothache.

Rue, a bitter woody perennial herb, is successful as an antidote for poison.

Those diseases of the breast which plague women can be made to disappear by the simple method of applying sedative cataplasms made of henbane. Henbane is a fetid Old World herb that contains a poison especially deadly to fowls; its leaves yield an extract used in medicine which has properties similar to those of belladonna.

Hebane is effective for irritable conditions; it can be used as a sedative in asthma or whooping cough.

For breast complaints of women, red clover is advised.

A sachet of belladonna applied to the stomach will ease the pain and convulsions of difficult childbirth. Belladonna is effective also for the gout and rheumatism.

If one has been bitten by a mad dog or by any venomous beast, he must drink wine in which verbena stalks have been boiled. Or he may apply to the wound directly leaves of the verbena plant.

Vervain and plantain are fine nerve tonics and can be used for feverish colds, fits, convulsions, and other complaints.

Take myrtle berries, dry and pound these and preserve with the white of egg. When applied in the form of a plaster to the mouth and the stomach, they prevent vomiting.

Myrtle leaves applied in compresses on the forehead, as well as the temples and feet, will bring calm and healing sleep to sufferers of fever. Stubborn colds and severe head pains can be relieved by inhaling the warm vapors of an infusion of myrtle leaves. Myrtle is effective as well for chest complaints and night sweats.

Abscesses which often prove mortal under the scalpel of surgery can be cured by bean flour, applied to the breast. Some use ordinary white flour and honey for the same purpose.

Marshmallow, a European perennial herb, is the best cure for abscess.

To cure abscess, apply any of the following, alone or in combination—red clover, slippery elm, and aconacia, but only these.

Onyx has properties similar to those of jasper; also, it increases saliva in boys and sometimes brings terrible shapes to the dreamer, from which the future can be divined. If applied to the eye, onyx acts as if alive, creeping about and removing noxious matter.

Opal is said to recreate the heart, to preserve from contagion in the air, and to be fine for weak eyes, making them quickly stronger.

Mugwort is a cure for gout and for fever.

Lodestone is universally known to possess diverse magical properties. If one is ill, one has to hold the lodestone in one's hands and shake it well. This will cure most wounds, snakebites, headaches, weak eyes; it will restore lost or weakened hearing.

Limachie is squeezed out of the head of a slug, which must be done the instant it is seen. This is an amulet highly effective against fever.

Red bezoar is known to have magical properties and is highly prized by all healers. It is a certain remedy against any poison and against contagion, whether it is taken internally or worn about the neck. There are nine varieties of bezoar and these differ greatly in composition, although all are found in the alimentary organs of animals; but generally these may be listed as those which consist mainly of mineral matter and those which consist mainly of organic matter. As to the origin of this stone, it is said that the stags of the Orient, when they became oppressed with years, fed upon certain serpents which restored their youth. But it was necessary to counteract this poison which was quickly absorbed into their systems, and for this purpose they plunged into running streams, keeping their heads above the water. A viscous fluid was distilled from their eyes, which was indurated by the sun's heat and formed bezoar. But whether such is true or not does not lessen the effect of these stones.

Emerald can be seen to be an excellent preservative against decay; it promotes childbirth, and arrests dysentery. Also it heals the bites of venomous animals. It is good for the eyes.

Live earthworms should be placed on an infected wound to cause a cure.

To prevent food poisoning, unicorn horn is most favorable.

Mummy powder is regarded by most physicians as powerful in curing disease. For the best results this must be from the mummy of a saint, or that of a very healthy young person who has recently been drowned, or has been killed by a fall. Somewhat less effective, but still to be desired, are thieves cut down from the gallows or beheaded rebels. As this flesh yet radiates life power it can regenerate failing spirits.

If a red-haired person will boil children's hair, this will produce an effective treatment for frost blisters.

Live toads are effective against bubonic pustules.

For very foul wounds, heap them with three handfuls of steamed pigeon's dung.

Moss grown on a skull is sometimes effective for hemorrhage.

Frog's eggs can be used as a disinfectant.

To bring forth the occult virtues in pearls, boil them in meat, then they will heal the quartan ague (malaria).

If pearls are bruised and taken with milk they will be beneficial to ulcers and will clear the voice. Worn in necklaces, these gems make their wearer chaste; as to their other properties, if they are crushed to a fine powder and mixed with milk, this drink will sweeten irritable temperaments; and crushed and mixed with sugar, they cure pestilential fevers.

Amber heals throat disease.

Cornelian which has been engraved with a man's figure holding a scepter in his hand will stop hemorrhages.

Engrave on red coral a man bearing a sword; this will heal hemorrhages.

Rely upon agapis to cure sting and venomous bite, if it is dipped in water and rubbed over the wounds.

Agate stone is the very best healing for scorpion bite or serpent bites.

Here is a recipe for restoring lost youth, which should be used every seven years: On the first day of this performance, a plaster made of one ounce of saffron, two of sandalwood (which also is red), half an ounce of red roses, a measure of aloe wood, and a similar quantity of fine amber should be placed on the heart during sleep. These shall have been ground into a very fine powder and mixed with a half pound of white purified wax, and then worked up with a sufficiency of oil of roses. This plaster must be taken off on wakening and then kept in a leaden box until used again. Now, the subject will live for some time on fowls, and these must be prepared in a certain way: for sanguine temperaments sixteen days is the prescribed time; for phlegmatics, twenty-five days are needed; and for melancholics, thirty days. He will obtain the number of fowls dictated by these times and by his appetite. These are to be kept in a large and airy yard with clear water but where there is no grass or

21

any other kind of food for them, because they are to be given only the food which is here described: Make this of as many vipers as there are fowls. These are to be whipped in a tub until their heads and tails fall off. Then they will be skinned, and they must be soaked in vinegar and rubbed with coarse salt shaken onto a piece of rough material. Cut into small pieces, they are thrown into a large pot with half a pound of rosemary and the same of fennel, calamint, and spignel, and add half a pound of cumin. With pure water fill the pot two-thirds full and then bring gently to a boil and continue until the vipers are cooked. Add then a quantity of wheat finely sifted and of sufficient quantity to feed the fowls for the length of time which has been previously determined according to the subject's temperament; this must be slowly poured in. This wheat is to be cooked until the essence of the reptiles has soaked in. The pot must be kept covered during this time lest the quality be affected, and it should be on a tripod so that it receives gentlest heat. The mixture will in time thicken, and if it is needed, a little water may be added to spare it burning. Finally, a preserve is added, which has been prepared ahead of citron, borage (a blue-flowered European herb), and rosemary, and a pound of fine sifted sugar. All of this is then poured in a new and air-tight jar. It must be taken every morning before breakfast and in the evenings before going to bed, half a spoonful. This will restore youth to even the oldest and most decrepit subject.

The iron that made the wound also will heal it.

If a patient suffers from a heart condition, he will cure it by eating a bull's heart.

Balasius stone, if it is bruised and drunk with a quantity of water, will relieve infirmities in the eyes; it will also tend to help disorders of the liver.

The euphrasia, or eyebright, is good for the eyes, as can be seen because it contains a black spot.

Emerald on which is engraved the likeness of the starling will strengthen weak eyes.

A spider hung around the neck will protect against ague, or heal that condition.

Aetites or aquilaeus is a precious stone which has diverse properties. It is composed of oxide of iron with silex and alumina, and some say it is found in the neck or in the stomach of the eagle, depending upon whom one asks. It will heal falling sickness and prevent untimely birth. To prevent abortion it ought to be worn bound on the arm; if it is bound on the thigh it will aid parturition.

A cock buried under the bed will cure a patient of epilepsy in most cases.

Chips from a gallows or from any place of execution make an effective amulet against ague.

The eel has many marvelous virtues. Let him die out of the water and steep his body in strong vinegar and the blood of a vulture, and place the whole under a dunghill. The composition will raise from the dead whatever is brought to it and give life as before. Also, anyone who eats the still-warm heart of an eel will be seized with a spirit of prophecy and will be able to foretell future events.

A bloodstone can be employed for stopping the flow of blood from a wound.

Pink amethyst prevents drunkenness when it is attached to the navel. But it must be set in a silver plaque or medal, and must have a bear engraved on it. If it is dipped in water, that water will cure sterility.

Bake a spider and wear it around the neck as a charm. Spiders and their webs cure the ague.

A poultice of peeled onions which is laid on the stomach or even under the armpits will cure anyone who has taken poison internally.

This is a remedy for enchantment: Lick the child's forehead in this manner, first upward, then across it, and then up again; then spit behind his back. This will be certain to work against a spell.

If you lick the forehead of a child with the tongue and you perceive a salt taste, this is certain proof that he has been fascinated, and the stronger the taste of salt, the more powerful the spell. If a death spell has been put, the tongue will be fairly burnt and only pure water will remove the briny taste.

To pull out a thorn easily, apply hare's fat.

The root of gladen (iris) is a remedy for the disease known as Elf Cake, which causes a hardness of the side; take a root of gladen and make powder of it and give the patient a half a spoonful of this powder in white wine and let him eat the same quantity in his pottage at the same time and it will help him.

If afflicted by nightmares, it is best to hang a stone over the bed, which stone has a natural hole in it wherein a string may be put through and so be hanged over the sufferer.

Oak apples will not fail to tell if a child has been bewitched, even by a clever witch. Place a basin of clean water under the child's cradle and drop into it three oak apples, keeping strict silence while doing so. If they sink, the child is surely fascinated, but if they do not, he is safe.

To cure a toothache, bore with a nail the tooth or the gum, after which drive the nail into an oak tree, the taller the better.

Amethyst expels poison when it is drunk in a potion.

To relieve asthma, take topaz in wine.

When drunk in a potion, amethyst will render the barren fruitful.

If a child has rupture, cure him by splitting an oak branch. Pass the child through the opening backward three times; if the splits afterward grow together the child will be cured, but if they do not the disease will continue.

This is an incantation to chase away nightmares:

> St. George, St. George, our lady's knight
> He walked by day so did he by night:
> Until such times as he her found,
> He her beat and he her bound,

Until her troth to him plight,
He would not come to her that night.

Take Roman vitriol six or eight ounces, beat it very small in a mortar, sift it through a fine sieve when the sun enters Leo; keep it in the heat of the sun by day and dry by night; if a person be wounded, apply it not to the wound but to the weapon by which he received it and the wound shall heal.

In West Country England it is known as a fact that warts can be easily cured by this method: steal a piece of meat and bury it. Just so long as the theft remains unconfessed and the meat rots, the warts will continue to disappear.

For the cure of warts, first burn a stick at one end in an open fireplace; take it out, but do not touch the charred end, and let the burnt portion cool. The black soot must be cooled, and it will be most effective if it is chilled by being put in snow, but this is not essential. Lay the burnt end then on the warts; only the other end of the stick can be held by the hand, the charred tip must touch only the warts that it is to cure. Then throw the entire stick in the fire, still taking care not to touch the charred end which now contains the essence of the warts. If it is touched, it will merely plant new warts.

This is the way to cure warts most effectively, and other cures are best forgotten. Split a bean. Cut the wart. Some say that blood should appear, but it will work either way in most cases. Half of the bean must be placed on the wart. If blood has come, some of it must be absorbed by the bean. Burn the other half of the bean to nothingness, but retain the half that has covered the wart, and wait for a moonless night. Then, on such a night, take the half of the bean to a crossroads, arriving there exactly at midnight. Here bury the bean, all the while chanting, "Down bean, off wart, come no more to bother me." This will remove the warts and they will not return.

You can stop an epileptic fit by reciting in a low voice over the stricken person this prayer: "Praeceptis salutaribus moniti, et divina institutione formati, audemus dicere. Pater noster . . . etc." Before you have finished the Lord's Prayer, the fit will have ended. Take care though to step over the man if he rolls on the ground, for if you touch him otherwise the illness will enter your own body as it leaves his. Another way to cure such a fit is to whisper the following into his right ear: "Gaspar fert mirrham, thus Melchior, Balthassar, aurum," and he will recover. If the man can point out the spot where first he fell to the ground, you can make his cure complete by driving three iron nails into the ground at that spot, each time pronouncing his name.

Arthritis is cured by taking hog's dung and charnell and putting them together and holding them in the left hand; and take a knife in the other hand and prick the medicine three times. And cast the medicine into the fire; and take the knife and make three pricks under a table, and let the knife stick there. And take three leaves of sage and as much of herb John or herb Grace and put them in ale and drink it last at night and first at morning; and this will ease the lameness infallibly.

To dispel worms in children, peach tree leaves should be preserved in vinegar with mint and alum and applied to the navel.

In times of plague chew burnet, any plant of the genus *Sanguisorba*, which will preserve you from contagion. Greater burnet is also useful for stopping hemorrhages.

Pound the flower of the marshmallow with turpentine and pork fat. Applied to the stomach, this cures inflammations of the womb. The root of the marshmallow plant, if it is infused in wine, prevents retention of the urine. If the seed of the marshmallow plant is pounded and kneaded into an ointment, this can be rubbed over the face and hands to insure against the stings of bees and wasps.

Royal comfrey, a plant of the genus *Symphytum*, is useful in bringing stillborn children from the womb. It will remove films from the eyes as well, if used in compresses. Royal comfrey is helpful to bones and ulcers, and its leaves are potent against inflammation.

Anet stalks can be cooked in oil and applied to the head to deliver one from insomnia.

Dill water is excellent for use in children's complaints, as flatulence.

To remove herpes (shingles) and other skin eruptions, one should grind leeks and mix with barley flour and oil.

28

If one is troubled with ulcers on feet and legs, plantain leaves will solve this, if they are pounded and applied as a poultice. To stop dysentery, pulverize seeds of plantain in wine, or preserve the leaves in vinegar. To cure dropsy, eat raw plantain leaves after dry bread, without taking a drink. The root of the fresh water plantain, when infused in wine, is useful in neutralizing opium poisoning and other narcotic effects.

Viburnum leaves in red wine are a certain cure for epilepsy. Also, for convulsions and spasms, viburnum or cramp bark is used.

Some women after giving birth are troubled by insatiable hunger. This can be easily remedied by pounding the leaves and tendrils of grape vines into a poultice which is applied to the stomach.

The grapestone can be roasted and pulverized and applied in poultice for the cure of dysentery.

Wormwood, cooked in wine and taken in small dosages, saves women from the danger of miscarriage.

Fumigations of wormwood boiled and taken in a hip bath will deliver a woman of a stillborn child.

Nettle seeds are effective against pleurisy and lung inflammations, for which they should be cooked in wine. The leaves of the nettle may also be pounded and applied to sores and wounds for the prevention of gangrene and to aid healing. If one suffers from mushroom poisoning, a decoction of the seeds of the nettle plant is advised.

A little nitre mixed with oil is effective against poisoning, especially mushroom poisoning.

Nettle seeds should be mixed with honey and sucked for goiter and for consumption.

Nettle has many outstanding properties. It is famed for sweetening the breath. Also, if one will hold a nettle stalk in his hand and a milfoil stalk which has been picked while the sun was passing through the Lion, he will be made completely impervious to fear. For gathering fish, a fine bait can be made from nettle juice and juice of snake root; when the hand is anointed with the blend and plunged into a body of water, it will attract whole schools of fishes, which can be easily captured.

For henbane poisoning, take the juice of the purslane, a plant of the family *Portulacaceae,* with a sweet wine.

Angelica in wine is a good cure for interior ulceration. If this plant is reduced to a powder, a pinch of it swallowed with wine before breakfast in the winter will guard one from winter epidemics. In the summer, the powder should be taken with rosewater to preserve from ills of that season.

For ulcers of the lung, an infusion of thistles is used. If the thistle root be powdered fine and applied it will cure ulcers of the breast.

Aloe juice with vinegar will invariably cure falling hair. Rosemary, southernwood, and citric acid are also prescribed for falling hair.

30

Chewed raw, purslane cures mouth ulcers. The seeds of the purslane, when crushed and eaten with honey, are effective against asthma.

Raspberry leaves are effective in treating mouth ulcers.

Angelica leaves, pulverized with rue and honey, will prevent rabies when applied to dog bites.

Agnus castus in a strong decoction will work to preserve chastity; moreover, with smallage and sage in salt water it results in a liniment for the back of the head which will restore those who have been in a coma.

To be completely safe from vipers or any venomous reptile, one need wear a belt of juniper, leeks, or verbena stalks.

It is most dangerous to the health of a woman if she accidentally suppress her monthly flows. If this happens, she must be made to take up her cycle again by heavy doses of fresh parsley-leaf tea.

If the monthly cycle is overdue, a woman must take finely chopped agrimony, feverfew, and parsley, which are mixed with oatmeal grits and all cooked with fresh pork. Only the liquid is to be drunk and the meat must be promptly thrown away and not allowed to linger in the brew.

Dissolve in the mouth three grains of sea salt and spread this over the teeth and gums with the tongue; the teeth will never decay if this is done each morning regularly.

For a pimply face, boil tobacco leaves and apply as a lotion. Echinacia is effective also.

For hemorrhage of the uterus, get seven oranges and stew their skins in three pints of water until there is only one pint of liquid left. Toss in a handful or two of sweet sugar. Take twelve spoonfuls of this three or four times each day.

Barberry is good against piles and liver difficulties. The root of this plant, or of the sorrel or the plantane, when worn around the neck, will cure scrofula and scrofulous tumors.

The elder plant, especially the flowers, will reduce inflammation; elder flowers mixed with honey and rye flour will cure erysipelas.

A cure for erysipelas is this: Take two ounces of the oil of roses and mix well together with three ounces of oil of water lilies and five ounces of warm milk, either goat or cow.

Cucumber is excellent against freckles and skin blotches.

If one is troubled by complexion, especially blotches or patches of redness, this is what to do. Take the gall of a cow and mix this with eggshells which have first been dissolved in vinegar.

There is a certain cure for unpleasant complexion which if followed will do the job. Goose droppings are to be soaked in wine. Every day for nine days a dose about the size of a walnut must be taken. This will also end jaundice.

Erotic dreams may have a debilitating effect. To be rid of them one must take a sheet of lead and cut it in the form of a cross, which is to be laid on the stomach.

People have been known to choke on fishbones, which can be very dangerous. The best thing to do if this should happen is to put your feet in a bowl of cold water. If bread crumbs stick in the throat, stuff the ears with the very same bread and there will be results.

The pains of childbirth can be reduced and even eliminated if one will take eagle's droppings and reduce them to powder, which is burnt over glowing embers to procure a fumigation. Another remedy is one ounce of raspberry leaf steeped in a pint of water; take this tea very often in large quantities after the first six months.

If one desires to make the hair grow, or to give the hair new life, he must roast bees. Take the ashes that result and mix these with mouse droppings. Infuse this blend in oil of roses. Now add the ash of roasted chestnuts, or roasted beans will do. Whatever part of the body you anoint with this, hair will grow there.

For dysentery or dropsy, goat's blood should be heated and drunk. For jaundice, take the gall of a goat, mix with honey and apply as an ointment. The gall of the goat dried and put on the stomach will cure or prevent inflammation there. For dysentery, roast a goat's head.

This is how you will cure a dropsical person without fail: Collect the droppings of a little unweaned dog and dry these and powder them. For nine days have the patient swallow this in any beverage, especially in wine. But if this is to work, the patient must not know the nature of this cure or it will lose its power.

You will bring a dead child from the womb if you apply to the stomach an ointment made from the juice of leeks, the fat of a he-goat, and the gall of a hare.

Liver ailments are best cured by taking a wolf's liver, which has been dried and crushed, in Madeira wine.

Your children will cut their teeth painlessly if you rub their gums with hens' brains.

You will ensure long life and good health if each day before dinner you will take two or three spoonfuls of honey.

If you will make a bracelet of raw silk and tie this about a child's wrist, he will not suffer from convulsions. But this danger is present until the period of the first teething is past, and so this bracelet must be kept on at all times and taken off only to be replaced by a clean one. Another protection against these convulsions is to steep the seeds of the male peony in white wine; then make a necklace of these on linen or hempen thread. The necklace must consist of an odd number of the seeds, not an even number.

Here is how you can make yourself appear to be ill and have a temporary feverishness. Cook a stag beetle in olive oil and rub the pulse with this ointment.

Jacinth cures dropsy.

To bring about a stoppage of bleeding, red coral is wanted.

Hyena stone cures quartan ague as well as the gout.

Sapphire cures inflammations of the eyes, especially when engraved with the image of a ram.

Antracites, antrachas, and anthrax are the same stone, which sparkles like fire. It cures imposthumes. It is girdled with a white veining. When it is smeared with oil it loses color, but if dipped in water it sparkles the more.

A Babylonian invocation to the goddess Tasmitu, to remove sickness or evil spells:
> I, son of ———, whose god is ———, whose goddess is ———,
> In the evil of an eclipse of the Moon, which in ——— month and on ——— day has taken place
> In the evil of the powers, of the portents, evil and not good, which are in my palace and my land,
> Have turned toward thee! I have established thee!
> Listen to the incantation! Before Nabu thy spouse, the lord, the prince, the first-born son of Isagila, intercede for me!
> May he hearken to my cry at the word of thy mouth!

May he remove my sighing, may he learn my
   supplication!
At his mighty word may god and goddess deal
   graciously with me!
May the sickness of my body be torn away!
May the groaning of my flesh be consumed!
May the consumption of my muscles be removed!
May the poisons that are upon me be loosed!
May the ban be torn away!

Akkadian incantation against disease:
   The wicked god, the wicked demon, the demon of
      the desert, the demon of the mountain, the
      demon of the sea, the demon of the marsh,
   Spirit of the heavens, conjure it!
   Spirit of the earth, conjure it!

Akkadian incantation for the plague:
   Incantation. Wicked demon, malignant plague,
   The spirit of the earth makes you leave his body.
   May the favorable genius, the good giant,
   The favorable demon,
   Come with the spirit of the earth.
   Incantation of the powerful, powerful, powerful
      God.
   Amen.

An Akkadian incantation against ulcers:
   That which does not go away,
   That which is not propitious,
   That which grows up,
   Ulcers of a bad kind,
   Poignant ulcers, enlarged ulcers, excoriated
      ulcers, ulcers,
   Ulcers which spread, malignant ulcers,
   Spirit of the heavens, conjure it!
   Spirit of the earth, conjure it!

An Akkadian conjuration against disease:
   The seven gods of the vast heavens,
   The seven gods of the great earth,
   The seven gods of the igneous spheres,
   These are the seven gods,
   The seven malevolent gods,
   The seven malevolent phantoms.
   Spirit of the heavens, conjure it!
   Spirit of the earth, conjure it!

An Assyrian healing spell:
   The man of Ea am I,
   The man of Damkina am I,
   The messenger of Marduk am I.
   My spell is the spell of Ea,
   My incantation is the incantation of Marduk,
   The circle of Ea is in my hand,
   The Tamarisk, the powerful weapon of Anu,
   In my hand I hold,
   The death spathe, mighty in decision,
   In my hand I hold.

A Chaldean magic formula against headache:
   Knot on the right and arrange flat in regular
     bands, on the left a woman's diadem:
   Divide it twice in seven little bands;
   Gird the head of the invalid with it:
   Gird the seat of life with it:
   Gird his hands and his feet:
   Seat him on his bed:
   Pour on him enchanted waters.

An Egyptian spell for poison or one suffering from any venomous bite: Fashion a hawk with two feathers on the head; this should be made of ivy wood and painted. Recite the spell below over it; open its mouth and offer it bread and beer and incense; then place it on the face of the victim. It will quickly repel the poison. This is the spell to be chanted:

"Flow out, thou poison, come forth upon the ground. Horus conjures thee, he cuts thee off, he spits thee out, and thou risest not up but fallest down. Thou art weak and not strong, a coward and dost not fight, blind and dost not see. Thou liftest not thy face. Thou art turned back and findest not thy way. Thou mournest and dost not rejoice. Thou creepest away and dost not appear. So speaketh Horus, efficacious of magic! The poison which was rejoicing, the hearts of multitudes grieve for it; Horus has slain it by his magic. He who mourned is in joy. Stand up, thou who wast prostrate. Horus has restored thee to life. He who came as one carried is gone forth of himself; Horus has overcome his bites. All men, when they behold Re, praise the son of Osiris. Turn back, thou snake, conjured is thy poison which was in any limb of ———, the son of ———. Behold, the magic of Horus is powerful against thee. Flow out, thou poison, come forth upon the ground."

A Roman spell to banish pain: Hang around the neck these words on a paper:
    An ant has no blood nor bile:
    Flee, uvula, lest a crab eat you.

A Roman incantation for dislocated bone:
    Huat hanat huat
    Ista pista sista
    Comiabo damnaustra.

CHAPTER TWO

In Matters of Love

Have you ever desired a woman who was unavailable to you because of your station, your physical appearance, or your economic situation? There are many women whose love is seemingly unobtainable. Have you gone to your bed and dreamed of a woman in all her loveliness, desiring her? She can be yours, if you are willing to use the correct spells. The following methods should be employed to gain the attention and favors of the woman of your choice:

Collect the following ingredients: two ounces of scammony (convolvulus), two ounces of Roman Cammomile, three ounces of cod bones, and three ounces of tortoise shell.

Heat the above ingredients together until they are melted into one. Allow to cool, then with mortar and pestle reduce the solution to a powdery mixture. Combine the entire concoction with five ounces of male beaver fat. Add thereto two ounces of oil of flowers made from blue scammony which you had earlier collected, and the collection of the flower should best be done in the first several days of the warm spring. Place this mixture into a boiling vat and reduce the composition down to one-quarter its content. Add to it an ounce of honey and several drops of dew, which you should gather from the seed of the poppy flower. Next, add several parts of opium and a few grains of tobacco gathered in the heat of a southern sun. Place this new mixture into a bottle, which must be sealed with the wax from altar candles, preferably virgin candles which have not as yet been lighted but have had their place on a shrine or altar for six days. Expose the container to the heat of the sun. Allow it to remain thus for ninety-five days. At the end of this period of time you take the container from its position under the sun and immediately place it in the cool temperature of a damp cellar. It should remain in the darkness of the cellar for one entire season under a coat of very fine builder's sand. When the frost thaws and disappears, when the first signs of spring are seen, remove the container and extract its contents. Pour this mixture which you have extracted into a pewter vessel which has been chilled over a block of ice. Be sure that the pewter vessel has been used before. Allow the substance to turn to ice and then allow it to thaw under the heat of a spring sun. When it is at body temperature, smear it over the genitals and retire to your bed. The woman of your choice will call upon you, or you will encounter her and speak with her within a fortnight. If you see her in the market square, do not be

40

afraid to speak with her. She will welcome your approach and will be seduced by your personality.

Another method which will make you irresistible to the opposite sex is: Venture to a river bed and catch a fat, green frog. Make a blazing fire and roast the legs of the frog until they are blackened. These will you reduce to a very fine ash. Carry with you a small piece of virgin parchment, onto which you sprinkle the fine ash (the final remains of the frog's legs). Fold the corners of the parchment toward each other and then fold in half so that the ash is imprisoned inside the creases of the virgin parchment. Place this small packet on a cord around your neck and wear it for thirty days. At the end of that time you will not be able to count the number of propositions women will offer you.

Still another method of making yourself irresistible to women is to gather up three laurel leaves on which you have printed in blood the names of the three archangels, Michael, Raphael, and Gabriel. Attach the leaves to the foot of the bed of your ladylove (if possible) or attach them to some part of her dress or person. She will be rendered senseless of everyone except you and will think of naught but you. You have but to command her and she will be yours.

The next method is to hint to the lady of your choice that you are adept at casting horoscopes and to ask whether she would like to have her chart prepared and read. All females are somewhat vain in nature, and not one will be able to resist the opportunity of being the center of attention. When you are confronted with the lady of your heart, pretend to read in generalities the stars and planets of her birthright. Make certain that during the conversation she looks you straight in the eye for several moments; hold her gaze steadily. When so affixed eye to eye, repeat in a low tone: "Kaphe, Kasita, non Kapheta et publica filii omnibus suis." If you conduct yourself in a believable manner and do not mock the ritual, the lady of your quest will be yours forever.

Another method is to be performed on the night prior to St. John's Day. You must go, prior to the rising of the sun, to a place where the Oenula Campana plant grows. Pick the plant and rub it briskly between the palms of your hands until the plant is shaped into a cylinder. Wrap this in a small piece of linen and place it in a pocket nearest your heart. Keep it there for a period of ten days, then grind it into a powder; then sprinkle it onto an arrangement of flowers or a box of sweets which you intend presenting to the lady of your desire. You will find that she is overwhelmed by your love.

Still another method is to take the liver and brains of a pigeon and the liver and brains of a blackbird. Allow them to turn dry, then crush them in a mortar with a pestle until they take the form of powder. This you can sprinkle into the ladylove's sweets, flowers, handkerchief, or any part or parcel of her makeup, and she will be yours evermore.

Another method: In the height of a brilliant sun on a midsummer day, go seek out some periwinkle

42

blossoms and brush them lightly with the powder from a poppy flower. To this add a mixture of musk and lime, and when the mixture has dried thoroughly reduce to a powder and sprinkle it on a bouquet of peonies. Send the flowers to the woman you desire and she will never forget you. You will stick in her mind as the object of her love for the rest of her days.

Still another method is to ask your ladylove for three of the hairs from her head. Plait them with three hairs from your own head. Make a small blaze in a brazier with the wood of the balsa plant. Into the fire cast your braid of hairs, uttering the following chant: "Ure igne sancti spiritus renes nostros et cor nostrum, Domine, Amen." This will render you and your love inseparable for the rest of your lives, and you will live in harmony and love and will beget many offspring.

If you wish to make a person remain faithful to you, simply steal a lock of her hair and sprinkle with ashes from an article of her clothing which you have purloined. Rub the hair and ash with honey taken from a wasp's nest. If you wish to keep her constant, never veering into unfaithfulness, simply repeat this small operation whenever necessary.

Collect the following: One dove's heart, one sparrow's liver, one swallow's womb, and one hare's kidney. Dry these ingredients together and reduce the whole affair to a very fine ash. Next, cut a small gash in the tip of your finger with an unused knifeblade and add several drops of blood to the dried mixture previously mentioned. Allow the blood to saturate the mixture and dry thoroughly. Feed it to the person you love, and her love will be everlasting.

So that the person of your choice will not stray in their affection for you, mix together some ambergris, powdered cypress wood, and the marrow from the bones of a wolf's left foot. Perfume the mixture with musk or some other heady scent and allow the person of your choice to inhale the aroma of this concoction. Her love for you will remain constant.

Do not take an established love for granted. There are many evil elements working against you, and do not forget this fact. It is most easy for two people to be alienated by the intercession of a third. Any practicing witch can sever a relationship merely by scattering a powder made of verbena on the place where the devoted couple lives. The verbena, however, must be gathered when the sun is passing through the sign of the Ram. This scattering of the verbena powder will cause much unhappiness and the closest of ties will be broken; the couple, once lovers, will become bitter enemies.

To find out if a girl is still virgin: Gather lily pollen and pulverize it. Sprinkle some of the powder into a refreshing drink and offer it to her without her knowledge of the powder having been deposited in said drink. If she has lost her virginity, she will be possessed by an uncontrollable urge to urinate—her bladder will feel filled to overflowing and she will not be able to contain herself.

44

Another method is to offer her a small lettuce seed. Ask her to inhale its slight odor. Make sure she smells at the seed until she can distinguish the odor. Again, if she no longer possesses her virginity, she will feel compelled to relieve herself. The desire to urinate will be uncontrollable.

To know if a woman is barren or frigid: Slay a new-born ram or a newly birthed hare and distill the blood. Mix a small quantity of the distilled blood in her tea or coffee. If she becomes extremely amorous and affectionate, the lady is not barren or frigid.

To know a woman's most intimate secrets: Search out a toad. Catch it while it is resting on a lily pad. Pull out the tongue of the toad and cast the toad over your left shoulder back into the water. When the woman of your choice has fallen asleep, place the toad's tongue over her heart. She will talk in her sleep and divulge to you her most intimate secrets.

Also, another method you can use is to sever the head from a toad and cut out the heart of a pigeon. Place both the toad's head and the pigeon's heart in a mortar and crush them with a pestle until they are a mash. Allow the mash to dry. Again work with mortar and pestle until the substance is reduced to a fine powder. Sprinkle some of the powder lightly over the stomach of the sleeping lady. She will talk to you in her sleep and will divulge to you all of her most intimate and personal secrets.

To see in a dream the woman you will marry: Collect coral from a south sea reef and reduce it to powder. Collect a small chunk of iron ore and reduce it also to powder. Collect the blood of one recently slain red chicken. Make a paste of the powdered coral, the powdered iron ore, and the blood of the chicken. Core a large fig and stuff the fig with the paste. This must then be wrapped in a small blue piece of silk and draped around the neck. Before retiring, cut down a small myrtle branch and place this under a goose-down pillow. Recite the following incantation: "Kyrie clementissime, qui Abrahae servo tuo dedisti uxorem, et filio ejus obedientissimo per admirabile signum indiscasti Rebeccam uxorem, indica mihi servo tuo quam nupturus sim uxorem, per mysterium tuorum Spiritum Baalibeth Assaibi Abumastith. Amen."

If the vision of the woman you are to marry has not appeared after repeating the above three evenings in succession, then it is obvious that you will never marry at all. However, usually the dream of a woman will occur after the first night, and it is reported that the vision sometimes occurs after the person has awakened and even during the hours of the high sun. It is not a process to be repeated too often, as you can render yourself sterile if you persist on conjuring up an image which is not destined to be yours.

If a woman wishes to envision the man she will marry: In the case of a woman who desires to see a vision of the man who will marry her, simply place a tiny branch from a poplar tree under her pillow, first wrapping it in one of her stockings and tying it with a white silken ribbon. Before she retires, she should rub into her temples the blood of a peewit and recite the following prayer (which is similar to that mentioned immediately prior hereto, but there is a slight difference, so take care which prayer is used): "Kyrie clementissime, qui Abrahae servo tuo dedisti uxorem, et filio ejus obedientissimo per admirabile signum indiscasti Rebeccam uxorem, indica mihi Ancillae tuae quem nuptura sim virum, per mysterium tuorum Spiritum Baalibeth Assaibi Abumastith. Amen."

To get a woman to tell you she loves you: Find a black agate set in white gold and veined with white. Wear this on a chain of gold around your neck for ten days. At the end of that time, offer the agate and chain to the lady of your choice.

To be assured of a person's love and affection: A very valuable stone to possess is the alectorine. It is a white stone about the size of a bean, and it grows in the ventricle of cocks which have been castrated at the age of three. The alectorine will produce a number of worthy results. It will protect you from your enemies—it will give you success and fame—it will assure you of a person's love and affection—it will provide you with wealth sufficient to allow you all the comforts of the world for the remainder of your years.

To write successful love letters: Obtain a piece of virgin parchment of the purest vellum and cover both sides of the parchment with the following invocation: "ADAMA, EVAH, even as the all-powerful Creator did unite you in the earthly Paradise with a holy, mutual, and indissoluble link, so may the heart of those to whom I write be favorable to me, and be able to refuse me nothing: * ELY * ELY * ELY."

The parchment should then be placed in a small earthenware bowl and burned to a crisp. Combine the ashes from the parchment with several drops of your own blood and a few drops of fresh cream. Search out a lodestone and pulverize it. Add the powder to the aforementioned mixture. Gather a goose quill and sharpen the point with an unused knife-blade, trimming the point to a writing tip. The substance should be a dark brown in color and should be fluid as ink. When you write your letters with this ink, the recipients will be unable to resist whatever you ask or offer. (It works as well for business letters as it does for love letters.)

To make a young girl dance: Mix together some wild marjoram, wild thyme, myrtle leaves, three walnut leaves, and several sprigs of fennel. In order to have a strong effect, these ingredients should be gathered on the first Friday of a new moon and should be sought in a lonely place immediately prior to the hour of midnight. Keep the articles for several days, then on the hottest day of the year allow them to dry under the noonday sun. Crush them with a mortar and pestle until they are pulverized. Make a sieve of silken cloth and pass the mixture through this sieve. When you wish the girl of your choice to dance for you against her will, simply ask her to sniff the powder like snuff, and a mere pinch of the powder will cause her to dance madly.

To make women adore you: The eating of olives by the woman of your choice, said olives having been sprinkled with the powder of the chayne herb and a grain of dried mustard seed, will cause the woman to idolize and adore you for the rest of her days.

To make women want to kiss you: Pick the leaves of the sage plant. This operation must be done when the sun is passing through the sign of Leo, the lion. Grind the leaves until they are reduced to a powder. This grinding must be done on a flat stone with another flat stone acting as the pestle. The stones must never have been used for this purpose before. Place the powder in a small glass vessel or vial. Bury this container in a heap of human feces and expose it to the heat of the sun for a period of not less than thirty days. At the end of the thirty-day period you will discover that the mixture has converted itself to a mass of writhing worms. Immediately build a blazing fire between stacks of red bricks. When the flames are high, place the worms on a small flat sheet of iron and fry the worms until they are burned to a crisp. Reduce this also to a powder by grinding between two flat stones (again, never before used for this purpose). Place in a well-sealed container and expose the container to the sun, placing it in the exact spot where the heap of human feces was located. After ten days, remove from the rays of the sun and place a grain or two of the powder under your tongue. Women, even those strange to you, will ask for your embrace. You will be rendered irresistible to all of the opposite sex.

Other results can be obtained by using this powder. Sprinkling it on your feet will bring you an unexpected journey which will result in many financial rewards; and putting the powder in the oil of a lamp will cause all who sit thereunder to imagine that the entire chamber is filled with vipers and monsters of every description.

As an amulet against the fascination of love: Take yourself to that place where the raising of donkeys is engaged in. Select a small new-born donkey and wait for it to roll itself in the dust. Collect a handful of the dust in which it rolled, and sprinkle some of this dust over your head and body. It will guard you against love's fascination.

Another means is to obtain a bone from the right side of a living toad. Extract any bone from the toad's right side and hang it around your neck. You will be tempted toward love, but will have strength to resist the temptation.

Still another amulet can be made from the liver of a chameleon. It will render you immune to the dart of Cupid's arrow.

To make someone fall in love with you: Squeeze the juice from the vervain and soak your hands with it. Rub it into the palms until the liquid is no longer discernible. Touch the man or woman you desire and they will be yours. If the juice of the vervain is not available to you, you can touch the person of your choice and recite the following words: "Bestarberto corrumpit viscera ejus mulieris" (which means: Bestarberto entices the inward parts of the woman). The individual will not be able to resist your advances.

To control lewdness: Gather the blossoms of the orchid plant. Crush the petals of the bloom until the juice flows. Rub the juice into the hands. Before allowing the solution to dry on the skin, touch the man or woman you want to restrain on the forehead. Lewd desires will disappear.

To make a man more passionate: If the man of your choice is not amorous enough, simply sprinkle powdered rhinoceros horn into his beverage. Another substance which is considered a strong aphrodisiac, for male or female, is the blossom of the periwinkle (blue only) reduced to a powder and sprinkled into food or drink. Still another is the black hellebore (the Christmas flower). Some believe that the fact that this blossom flourishes during the winter season makes it strong in character, and therefore it will give virility and strength to all who eat of its petals.

To retain an erection: If the man of your choice fails to retain his erection, it is advisable to bury the foot of a badger underneath the mattress on which he is lying. According to the gypsies, this will give him the stamina to perform as long and as often as you desire.

Two Sanskrit spells for gaining a man's love, from the Atharva Veda:
"I am possessed by burning love for this man: and this love comes to me from Apsaras, who is victorious ever. Let the man yearn for me, desire me, let his desire burn for me! Let this love come forth from the spirit and enter him.
"Let him desire me as nothing has been desired before! I love him, want him. He must feel this same desire for me!
"O Maruts, let him become filled with love. O

Spirit of the Air, fill him with love. O Agni, let him burn with love for me!"

"By the power and Laws of Varuna I invoke the burning force of love, in thee, for thee. The desire, the potent love spirit which all the gods have created in the waters, this I invoke, this I employ, to secure thy love for me!
"Indrani has magnetized the waters with this love force.
"And it is that, by Varuna's Laws, that I cause to burn!
"Thou wilt love me, with a burning desire."

Take a band of linen of sixteen threads, four of which are white, four green, four blue, and four red, and make them into one band and stain them with the blood of a hoopoe; bind it with a scarab in its attitude of the Sun God drowned, being wrapped in byssus, and bind it to the body of the boy whom you want to charm with a love spell, and it will work its magic at once on him.

CHAPTER THREE

The Making of Mischief

The literature on magic, witchcraft, and the black arts contains few specific formulas for doing harm to others, and for good reason. For a witch to write down such instructions would be to invite their retaliatory use on her own person. At one recent informal get-together, a self-styled "witch" carried with her a large volume purported to be her grimoire, the book of spells and charms a witch uses much like a recipe book. When the subject of death-spells came up, she opened her book to such a spell and proceeded to pass it about the room. The fact that she did so marked her at once as a charlatan, for no real witch, believing in the reality of such a spell, would let it fall into other hands.

Extant literature, however, does reveal some evil charms as well as a few means of creating simple mischief. And there are some natural items, such as certain stones, which are said to possess unpleasant qualities.

A black cock thrown into the air produces thunder and lightning.

Polytrix stone is inauspicious. It will cause the hair to fall out of the head of the person who has it about him.

To raise storms, the coven should hit a stone with a wet rag whilst reciting this charm:
>I knock this rag upon this stone
>To raise the wind in the Devil's name:
>It shall not lie, until I please again.

If some powdered lodestone is sprinkled on chafing dishes filled with blazing coals and placed at the four corners of a house, as soon as vapors rise those in the house will be seized with vertigo; it will seem to them that the ground is shaking, and they will look for the house to fall down about them.

He who would enjoy diabolical dreams must rub his eyelids with blood of bat before sleeping and put under his pillow leaves of laurel.

If children are put in a cradle of elderwood, they cannot sleep well and are ever in danger of falling out of it.

It is unlucky for sailors to whistle whilst on a ship, for thus they raise the whistling winds.

If a man wishes to cast a bewitchment, he must consecrate some nails to evil. Then he must nail them crosswise above the foot imprint of the one who is to suffer. The same can be brought about if an animal is selected to represent the intended, and some of his hair or his garments are attached to it. Then give it the name and afterward torture it, which can be accomplished by driving of nails or red-hot pins or even thorns into the body, to the rhythm of maledictions.

If one will select a fat toad, and will baptise it with the name of one's enemy, and will make it swallow a host both consecrated and execrated, then tie it with hairs of the intended victim upon which one has first spat and bury this creature at the threshold of the bewitched one's door, it will issue thence as nightmare and vampire and will ever torment the enemy.

Anyone can possess the power to make another dance wildly, no matter how sober they be. This you will do by writing with a bat's blood on virgin parchment the words, Sator Arepo Tenet Opera Rotas. Put this parchment under the threshold of your house.

The gall of the common crow can make the bravest man fearful and will not fail to drive him from that spot wherein it is placed.

There is an art called envoutment, that is to say, making an enemy die by means invisible; and this is done by two principal spells: First procure a little of the urine of that one whom you have sworn to kill with implacable hatred, then buy a common hen's egg but without haggling over its price. Go at night on either a Saturday or a Tuesday to some field or wood removed from human habitation and where these acts will not be disturbed nor discovered. A dark lantern may be carried if there is no moonlight. When a suitable place has been found, you must make a circular incision at the broadest end of the egg, through which you will extract the white only, leaving the yolk within. The egg must then be filled up again with the urine which you have brought along, and the name of the condemned person pronounced. Then the opening must be closed with a piece of virgin parchment. When all this is finished, you will bury the egg and in leaving will be careful never to look back. This egg will soon begin to rot, and when it does, the condemned person will be attacked by jaundice. There will be no cure for this illness save that the egg be taken from the earth and burned, and this by the hands of the same one who buried it. But if it be allowed to rot completely, that man upon whom the spell was cast will die within the year, and nothing can save him.

Yet another method: on a Saturday one will buy the heart of an ox, without haggling over the price. This he will take to a field, or a deserted cemetery, or a copse. Here he will dig a deep hole, and in this put a layer of quicklime, and upon the quicklime place the ox's heart. This he will prick as often as he wishes, each time pronouncing the name of the intended victim. He will finish the business by reciting the first chapter of the Gospel according to St. John. After this he must go away in complete silence, and even should he meet someone he must not speak. Each day thereafter he must again recite the Gospel before breakfast, keeping always in mind the desire to be avenged. In a short while the bewitched person will start to feel internal pains.

These will become more and more severe and will be at their worst at the time when one is thinking upon the revenge. And if this is kept up, the victim will eventually die of consumption.

Take a needle which has been used for sewing up a dead man's winding sheet. While whispering the words, "Coridal, Nerdac, Degon," place the needle under a table. Thereafter a mysterious and unbearable horror will prevent all from eating at the table.

If a walking toad be buried in the name of a certain person, and the one casting the spell circle round it, the one whose name was pronounced will not rest by day or night until he find it and burn it.

A magnet that has been rubbed in leek will lose its powers of attraction, be they ever so strong.

Make from pure wax two figures, one in the likeness of a man and the other a woman. Over them sprinkle lightly human blood, and fill up the heads with poppy seeds. Then fling them upon the ground and little men and women will appear, as many as there were seeds in the heads.

Guests seated around a table can be made to come to blows. One must take all four feet of a mole and put them under the cloth unnoticed. Those at the table will not fail to quarrel violently.

Periwinkle stalks have violent natures. If they are dried and reduced to powder, and then mixed with flowers of sulphur and thrown into a pond, the fish will die; and if an ox swallows it, he will die.

There is a spell that can be made. Take centaury and reduce it to powder. Add a peewit's blood and some honey, and mix this into the oil of a lamp. Those who gather around the lamp will suffer strange imaginings. They will think that they have stretched to monstrous proportions and that their heads are bumping against the sky. If this same substance be kept in a vial and shaken out under the nose of another, that one will be stricken with a sudden inexplicable horror and will run away.

To prevent a person from leaving a room, obtain the heart of a wolf and the heart of a horse. Dry these and reduce them together to a powder. Sprinkle this powder on the ground outside of the room. So long as the powder remains there, the one upon whom the spell is cast will be unable to leave the room.

If one wishes to make a tree barren he must take rose and mustard seeds and a polecat foot and reduce these to a fine powder. With this powder he will sprinkle any tree when it is blossoming and it will not bear any fruit. If one puts this same powder into a lamp, those who gather around it will appear as negroes to one another. If the same powder is blended with olive oil and some of the flowers of sulphur, when the walls of a room are anointed with it they will seem to be aflame.

Whoever takes mistletoe from an oak and hangs it with the wing of a swallow on any tree, all the swallows of the neighborhood will gather at that place.

To prevent sleep, use a piece of red string that has never been used before, and with it hang up in the house the feathers from the right wing of a blackbird. No one will find sleep in that room.

If you rub the sheets of a bed with very fine powdered alum, no one will be able to sleep in the room.

One of the bitterest of all curses is the Reversed Journey. This is how it is done. The person goes to chapel and makes the Journey (the Stations of the Cross) backwards. He begins the Journey at the last picture, Number Fourteen, and he finishes at the first picture. All the time he must invoke the Devil and ask this Prince to send bad luck and dire misfortune upon the enemy.

This is a charm to harm another's cows: While the sun is passing through the sign of the Lion, pick a lily and mix it with laurel juice. Place these under a layer of dung. They will produce worms which must be collected and ground to a powder. If this is thrown into a jugful of milk which is then placed in a byre, after first being covered with a piece of cowhide, all those cows in the byre who have the same color as the piece of hide will go dry. This same powder can be used in another way: if it is put in one's clothes or in his bed, that one will not be able to sleep until the powder is removed.

If stalks of henbane are wrapped in the skin of a young hare and buried at a crossroads, all of the dogs of the neighbourhood will collect there and will remain and not be driven away until the spell has been removed.

Take a new knife and with it cut asunder a lemon, at the same time speaking words of hatred and malice against an enemy. The enemy, no matter at what distance he be, will feel a certain cutting anguish of the heart and a cold chilliness throughout his body.

If someone has offended you and you wish to revenge yourself upon him, this is how it is done: On a Saturday, go before sunrise and cut a branch from a year-old hazel which has never before been touched by hand. While doing so, say: "I cut you, branch grown this summer, in the name of (and here you use the name of your intended victim) whom I wish to punish." Once you are home again, spread a new wool cloth on a new table which has never before been used, saying thrice: In nomine Patris * et Filii * et Spiritus * sancti, et in cute Droch * Mirroch * Esenaroth * Betu * Baroch * Maaroth *. At each place indicated * you must make the sign of the cross. When this invocation has been repeated thrice, say: "Holy Trinity, punish him who has done evil towards me and deliver me from this evil by thy great justice. * Elion * Elion * Esmaria. Amen." On the final word, begin to beat on the table with your stick. Your victim will simultaneously receive invisible blows, as many as you care to deliver to the table.

A simple method of avenging oneself: On a Friday, obtain from the person who has harmed you a hair belonging to him. Each day for nine days make a knot in this hair. On the ninth day wrap this knotted hair in virgin parchment and beat it. Each blow will be felt by your victim.

With this liquor, men can be made as raging and furious as a bear and can even be made to imagine themselves turned into that animal. First, dissolve or boil the brains and heart of a bear in new wine. Then give any person this drink out of the skull of the beast, and while this draught acts in him he will think himself a bear and perceive all others as the same animal. Nor can he be cured or changed of mind until the strength of the liquor has entirely exhausted itself.

An evil charm can be made in the following way: In the first mansion of the moon, you must make in an iron ring the image of a black man, in a garment of hair and girdled round, who is casting a small lance with his right hand. If this is sealed in black wax and perfumed with liquid storax (a balsam obtained from the bark of an Asiatic tree), you can wish for evil to befall and it will do so.

The Fattura Della Morte (death-maker) of Naples: A large green lemon must be selected, into which are stuck some two dozen or so great nails, and about these is intricately twined a thread of colored yarn. This is then smoked over a brazier, and the caster at the same time utters evil prayers. This is among the foulest of charms, and may even bring death.

The English Witches' Ladder, or Italian Ghirlanda Delle Streghe: Knot a cord at regular intervals, and in each knot tie the feather of a black hen. Lay a curse upon it. It is a fatal talisman of death.

The Spell of the Black Hen is made in the following manner: Paint the figure of a hen black and stuff this with hair. It will be best if this includes some hair of the victim or some parings of his nails. Then throw this into the water to rot away. The hen may also be knitted of black wool or may be cut out of black cloth. Also, black pins may be stuck into it.

This is the formula for making a storm: I conjure my Satan and Beelzebub; come and draw up the water, making a solid cloud in the sky; let the icy North Wind come and cause ice; let the ice become particles and fall, driven by the wind, upon dwellings, and fields, and vineyards; let the water descend like unto a cloudburst.

Add nail filings—that is, nail dust—to a drink to make a person ill. This will work only with liquor and not beer.

A sure method of disposing of an enemy requires the conjuring up of the victim's image in a bucket of water. When the image appears, the sorcerer stabs it with a knife. The image will turn blood-red as the victim dies.

Ill can be brought to a person. Make a likeness of wax and wrap this in some cloth belonging to the victim. Beginning with the chief of the coven or group, each member must handle the figure and say over it, "This is (the name of the victim), ordered to be consumed at the instance of ———," here ending with their own names or the name of the person requesting the spell be cast.

Here is a powerful spell. Stick a knife into the wall and hang from this a tag or label. Draw and stroke this tag after the manner of milking a cow's udder. In this manner you will obtain the milk of the kine of the person you wish to bewitch. That person will be plagued and may even die from it.

In order to turn over a haycart, inscribe on it the names of evil spirits.

In the summer, a person should not wash his shirt on Friday, nor wash his person, as this will ensure storms.

To raise storms, throw a stone and a woman's hair into running water or a pool. If pine fragments are added, frost will be raised.

To raise winds, call the East Wind while blowing through a reed.

The crops of another can be ruined by a coven. To do this, yoke a tiny model plough with toads, with traces made from dog grass and a ram's horn. Take the plough twice around the field, accompanied by the entire coven. One should hold the plough, and the chief of the group should lead in this. Marching all the while, the group must pray for the field to be barren. The farmer will afterward get no good from the field, but it will produce only weeds and thorns.

There are certain methods of affecting the weather, and the principal ones are these: Tie three knots on a string hanging at a whip. When the first of these is loosened, it will raise tolerable winds. If a second is loosed as well, the wind will be more violent. But if the third is loosed, it will raise tempests. Also, a devout witch can beat water in a pond with a rod, whereupon the water will rise to form clouds and these can be directed to make lightning, hail, or rain, whichever is desired. Another method is to make a hole in a field and urinate into it, afterward stirring up the mud, which will produce rain. The same will result if a sacrificial pullet is thrown into the air while one at the same moment calls upon the Devil to produce a storm. Also, if one casts a flint stone over the left shoulder toward the west, this will cause rain; so will throwing a little sea sand into the air; or wetting a broom and shaking it; or digging a hole and pouring water in it; or burying sage until it turns rotten; or laying sticks on the dry bank of a river; or boiling hog bristles. Also, if eggs are boiled in a pail of water, or if a wet rag is beat against a stone, or if a baby is boiled in a cauldron, or if one whistles on a ship, it will produce rain and even storms. The best method is to take a cat and christen it, and afterward bind to each part of that cat the chiefest part of a dead man and several of the joints out of his body. Then throw the cat into the sea. This will not fail to affect the weather.

According to the ancients, the direst mischief one can cause is the death of one's enemy. In order to accomplish this, the witch must gather several lizards of the two-tailed variety and must place them in a small vat of boiling oil. The lizards are then cooked most thoroughly, and when the oil is cooled and the lizards cooked almost into nothingness, the man who is to die is anointed with the oil. Death will follow within a comparatively short period of time.

Another curse that was popular with the ancients was one whereby the enemy would never again spend a peaceful day. According to a medieval grimoire, the *Key of Solomon*, the spell-caster would recite the following curse and the victim would become bewitched:

"Whence hast thou flown, O great Adonai, Eloim, Ariel, Concisore, Seductore, Seminatore? O almighty, ye who create and nurture hatreds and prolong hostilities: Come unto me who have conjured you up for this work. Ye must fulfill the duty I place upon you. (The witch must hold up a platter of various foods.) Evil spirits of darkness, I command that when (here the witch must insert the name of the victim) eats of these foods, or touches same or others of their kind, then (name of victim) shall ne'er find solitude in this world or any world beyond this."

The following is a curse for separating husband and wife: Write upon a new-laid egg in a Nazarene cemetery, "I conjure you, luminaries of heaven and earth, as the heavens are separated from the earth, so separate and divide (name of husband) from (name of wife); and separate them from one another as life is separated from death, and sea from dry land, and water from fire, and mountain from vale, and night from day, and light from darkness, and the sun from the moon, thus separate (name of husband) from (name of husband)'s wife; and sep-

65

arate them from one another in the name of the twelve hours of the day, and the three watches of the night, and the seven days of the week, and the thirty days of the month, and the seven years of Shemittah, and the fifty years of Jubilee, on every day, in the name of the evil angel Imsmael, and in the name of the angel Iabiel, and in the name of the angel Drmiel, and in the name of the angel Zahbuk, and in the name of the angel Ataf, and in the name of the angel Zhsmael, and in the name of the angel Zsniel who presides over pains, sharp pains, inflammation, and dropsy; and separate (name of husband) from his wife (name), make them depart from one another, and that they should not comfort one another, swiftly and quickly." [According to H. E. Wedeck, this spell was found in *The Sword of Moses,* an ancient book of magic containing mystical names, formulas, and recipes along with eschatological doctrines. *The Sword of Moses* was first published from a unique manuscript by Dr. M. Gaster, London, 1896.]

CHAPTER FOUR

The Divining Arts

Of all the more or less magical arts, none has held such fascination as that of foretelling the future. No class or society of man has ever been free from the desire to do so. In the most primitive dwellings and the most modern skyscrapers, man has pondered the mysterious future, and from his musings have come such a multitude of divinatory arts that they could not be contained in any single volume. Entire libraries could be compiled on the subject of astrology alone (a subject which, because of its complexity and size, we have had to omit here). Tarot, palmistry, the reading of dreams —these and other methods have their devotees. Probably no man is so completely skeptical that he will not allow his glance to linger for a second or two upon the patterns of the tea leaves in his cup or wonder, if only fleetingly, about the lines on his hand.

We wonder not only about the future and what it will bring, but about all sorts of knowledge not readily available to us. Almost all of us have plucked the leaves of a plant or the petals of a daisy, saying, "He loves me, he loves me not." We live in a world whose secrets are many and yield to us only reluctantly, if at all. But we remain stubbornly certain that somewhere in that world is an object, a phrase, a key, that will reveal all of those secrets to us, make us privy to all that is and has been and will be. And perhaps—just perhaps—someday man will find that key. Perhaps he already has.

From the eye of the Hyena one can take a multicolored stone called the Hyena stone. Put under the tongue, it enables its possessor to tell future events. It cures the gout and quartan ague as well.

Do you wish to find out how a sick person will fare, and how his illness will end? Take a sprig of verbena in your left hand and come up to his sickbed, asking him how he feels. Should he say, "Unwell," he will improve. But if he says, "Well," then he is in danger of death. The celandine has a similar power, according to some. You must put a stalk of this plant on the patient's head. If he is near recovery he will weep aloud; but if he is near death he will burst into song.

Hamn is a sacred stone not unlike gold, which is shaped like the horn of a ram. If its owner is a contemplative man, it will give his mind a representation of all divine things.

Amandinus is a many-colored stone. It enables its owner to answer any question concerning dreams or mysteries.

68

It will be easy to foretell future events if one has lignite bound upon the forehead.

Celonitis or celontes is a most wonderful stone which is found in the tortoise and has the property of resisting fire. It has healing virtues similar to the asinius. If carried under the tongue on the day of the new moon and for fifteen days thereafter during the lunar ascension, it inspires the owner to foretell the events of the future every day from the rising of the sun to six o'clock; and in the decrease during the intervening hours.

Crystal can produce visions.

Magicians and sorcerers employ an anathema to discover thieves, witches, enemies, and such. Some limpid water is brought, and in it are boiled as many pebbles as there are persons suspected in the matter. These pebbles are then given the names of the suspected persons, after which they are buried under the doorstep over which the suspects are to pass, and a plate of tin is attached which says: "Christ is conqueror; Christ is king; Christ is master." The stones are removed at sunrise and that one named for the guilty person is hot and glowing. But it is known that the Devil is malicious, and we cannot trust upon this evidence alone. The seven penitential psalms must then be said, with the Litanies of the Saints, and the prayers of exorcism must be pronounced against the thief or sorcerer. Then write his name in a circular figure and drive in above it a triangular brass nail with a hammer the handle of which is cypress. While doing this, say, "Thou art just, Lord, and just are thy judgments." At this the thief will reveal himself with a loud cry.

If an anathema has been pronounced by a wizard and one wishes to escape its effects and send it back upon the one who cast it, it is done thus. On Saturday, before sunrise, take the branch of a hazel tree of one year and recite the following prayer: "I cut thee, branch of this year, in the name of him whom I wish to wound as I wound thee." Then the branch is laid upon the table and other prayers are said, which must end with, "Holy Trinity, punish him who has done this evil and take him from among us by thy great justice, that the sorcerer or sorceress may be anathema and we safe."

On All Hallows' Eve, young men and maids often engage in the ceremony of pulling the green kail. They go hand in hand with their eyes shut into the garden of a bachelor or spinster and there pull up the first kail stalks they espy. If these prove to be of stately growth and straight of stem, with plenty of dirt at their roots, the future husband or wife will be young and good-looking and rich in proportion. But should the stalks they pull be crooked or small or have little earth at their roots, the future spouses will lack looks and fortune. They can taste of the stem, too, and if it is sweet to the taste, so will be the temperament of the future spouse, but if it tastes sour, so will be the disposition. Lastly, these stalks are put above the doors of the houses, and the first person to pass under will have the same Christian name as the future husband or wife.

An axe can provide an excellent way of detecting robbers. The hatchet must be cast on the ground, head down, with the handle perpendicular in the air. All those present must then dance around and around it in a ring until the handle totters and the axe falls over. The end of the handle will indicate the direction in which the thief must be sought. There are some who say that if this is to succeed the head of the axe must be stuck in a round pot, but as Delancre says, this is absurd; for how could the axe be fixed in a round pot, any more than the pot could be patched up if the axe breaks it to pieces? This is probably only superstition and not necessary to the divining.

In Hungary, whoever has been robbed and wishes to name the thief must take a black hen and fast along with it for nine Fridays. Then either the thief will bring back what was stolen, or he will die. This is known as taking up a black fast against one.

There is a method whereby it can be discerned whether a person is innocent of sorcery, by weighing him up against the great Bible in the church. If the person weighs less than the Bible, he is innocent.

It is a good omen when burnable objects tossed into a fire do not ignite.

Some persons wish to hold converse with spirits, and of all the methods prescribed for doing so, here is a most effective one. It must be done in the day and hour of Mercury, that is, the 1st, 8th, 15th or 22nd. When the right night has come, the sorcerer shall take a rod, a goatskin, a bloodstone, two crowns of vervain, and two candlesticks with candles; also new steel and two new flints, some wood to make a fire, half a bottle of brandy, incense and

71

camphor, and four nails taken from the coffin of a dead child. The ceremony must be done by either one or three persons, two is unfortunate. In either case, only one person may address the spirit. The Kabbalistic circle should be formed of strips of kidskin fastened down by four nails. The bloodstone is used to trace a triangle within the circle, starting at the eastern point. In like manner the letters a,e,a, and j must be drawn, also the name of the Saviour between two crosses. The candles and the crowns of vervain are put in the left and right sides of the triangle and within the circle, and they are lighted, as is the brazier, the fire being fed with brandy and camphor. A prayer must be repeated. It is essential too that the sorcerer have no alloyed metal about him except a gold or a silver coin wrapped in paper. This must be cast to the spirit when he appears outside the circle. Conjure the spirit three times. If the spirit does not then appear, plunge the two ends of the rod into the brazier's flames. This is known as the rite of Lucifuge, and it is the demon Lucifuge Rofocale who is invoked.

Here is the custom of eating the apple at the glass, which is done on All Hallows' Eve. You must take an apple and when the clock strikes twelve go into a room where there is a glass. You should be alone. Cut up the apple into small pieces. One of these should be thrown over your left shoulder. Then advance to the mirror without looking behind you. Eat the rest of the apple while combing your hair. As you do so, the face of the person you are going to marry will appear peeping over your left shoulder.

To perform cleidomancy, the sun or the moon must be in Virgo. Write the name of a supposed thief on a key and tie the key to a Bible. Hang both upon the nail of the ring finger of a virgin. If the key and book turn while she prays, the name is right; but if they remain stationary it is wrong. More fearful effects can be produced if the seven psalms with litanies and sacred prayers are added. Not only do the book and key turn in this case, but the impression of the key can be found upon the thief's person, or else he may lose an eye. Still another method of doing this is to place the key to the street door on the Fiftieth Psalm and close the book, fastening it tightly with the garter of a maid. Then suspend it on a nail and it will turn when the name of the thief is said aloud. Some people suspend the Bible between two persons who hold the ring of the key with their forefingers.

The cawing of a crow is an omen of evil.

For crystal-gazing one wants a perfect sphere, free from any speck or flaw and highly polished, contained in a stand of polished ebony (which is best) or else ivory or boxwood. Among the Hindus, a cup of treacle or a pool of ink is made to serve the same purpose. The one practising the invocations must be a man of pure life and religious bent. For the few days beforehand he must make frequent ablutions and subject himself to strict religious discipline with prayer and with fasting. Both the crystal and the stand on which it rests are to be inscribed with sacred characters, and so must be the floor of the room in which the invocation is to take place. A quiet retired spot is wanted for the purpose, where the magician need fear no disturbance. The mental attitude of the magician is important; perfect faith is essential. If he is accompanied by one or two friends, they must abide by the same rules and conditions absolutely. Choose the time of the invocation according to the position in the heavens of the various planets, all preparations having been made during the moon's increase. All of those instruments used for the invocations—the sword, rod, and compasses, the fire and the perfume to be burned, and the crystal itself—must be consecrated or charged prior to the ceremony. During the invocation the magician faces the east and summons the spirit he desires from the crystal. Magic circles should have been inscribed on the floor, and it is advised that the crystallomancer remain inside these for some time after the spirit has been dismissed.

A branch of laurel is thrown on the fire. If it crackles in burning it is a good sign, but if it burns without doing so the prognostication is false.

The howling of dogs at night presages death to those who are ill.

The chattering of a magpie may be considered a sure omen of evil.

Capture a ladybird. Bid it fly north, south, east, or west, in the direction in which your lover lives. It will fly in the direction of your future husband or wife.

Napellus is a plant that has narcotic properties. If one prepares the root roughly and tastes it with the tongue, in a very short while the center of thought and intellect will seem to become situated in the pit of the stomach. An unusual clarity and distinctness of thought will render the experience pleasant, and visions will occur.

A pearl can be covered with a vase and placed near the fire, and over it are pronounced the names of persons who are suspected of evil. When the name of the guilty party is said, the pearl will bound upward and pierce the bottom of the vase.

Onimancy, or the observation of the angel Uriel, is thus performed: Upon the nails of the right hand of an unpolluted boy or a young virgin, or the palm of the hand of such, put some of the oil of olive, or what is still better, oil of walnut, mingled with tallow or blacking. If money or things hidden in the earth are sought, the face of the child must be turned toward the east. If crime be inquired into or the knowledge of a person out of affection, toward the south. Then the child should repeat the seventy-two verses of the Psalms, which the Hebrew Kabbalist collected for the Urim and Thummim. These will be found in the third book of Reuclin on the Kabbalistical art and in a treatise *de verbo mirifico.* In each of these verses occurs the venerable name of four letters, and the three-lettered name of the seventy-two angels, which are referred to the inquisitive name Schemhammaphoras, which was hidden in the folds of the lining of the tippet of the high priest. When the curious student has done thus much he shall see wonders.

To dream of pearls means many tears.

If a young lass has several suitors and wishes to know which of them will turn out to be her husband, she will pick a rose leaf for each of the men and name a leaf after each lover, and watch them until they sink; the last to sink will be her future husband.

The cry of the screech-owl at midnight means evil.

The mirror of Solomon is a fine means of divination. To prepare this instrument, take a shining and highly polished plate of fine steel which is somewhat concave, and with the blood of a white pigeon inscribe at the four corners the names Jehovah, Eloym, Metratron, Adonay. Place the mirror in a clean white cloth, and when you behold a new moon during the first hour after a sunset, repeat a prayer that the angel Anael may command and ordain his companions to act as they are instructed— that is, to assist the magician in divining. Cast upon the coals a suitable perfume, and at this time utter a prayer. Repeat this thrice, then breathe upon the mirror and now invoke the angel Anael. Then make the sign of the cross upon the mirror and upon the operator for forty-five days in succession. At the end of the period Anael will appear in the form of a beautiful child and accomplish the magician's wishes. Sometimes he appears as early as the fourteenth day, according to whether the magician is devout and fervent in his prayers. The perfume used in evoking him is saffron.

In Devonshire, the maidens pluck yarrow from a man's grave. They place this under their pillows and repeat rhymes, and as a result their true loves appear to them in their dreams and seem altogether real.

A red rose will not bloom over a grave, even one that is concealed cleverly or very old.

Questions on which one wishes to be enlightened may be written on fig leaves. If the leaf dries quickly after the appeal to the diviner, it is an evil omen; but if it dries slowly it is a good omen.

If a white rose comes to bloom in autumn it is a token of an early marriage.

Fling a few jasmine or poppy seeds upon burning coals and they will provide omens; if the smoke rises lightly and ascends straight into the heavens it is well. But if it hangs about low it is certainly a bad omen.

Should a calandria bird follow you or display an unusual interest in your house, it is an infallible sign of some impending disaster.

A midwife can determine whether a newborn infant will live or die simply by licking his skin. If the skin tastes very salty, he will die. If he tastes of nothing at all, he will live.

If verbena is burnt during invocations and predictions, it will drive away evil spirits and attract good influences.

To determine the culprit in cases of theft, use this method: Have all the suspects line up and stick out their tongues. Then place a small frog on each tongue. If the frog jumps off the tongue to the ground, that man is innocent. But if the frog attempts to jump down the throat, that man is guilty.

To find water, grasp a forked hazel branch in both hands and walk slowly over the ground. When you pass over the area where water flows the stick will bend downward and vibrate violently.

To practice alectryomancy a circle is traced on the ground and divided into sections corresponding to the letters of the alphabet. These are sprinkled equally with grain and a cock is released. The sections in which he pecks will spell out the desired message. It must be explained, though, that the observor must be careful to replace the grains as quickly as they are pecked out, in case the same letter is required more than once.

Beryl is a good medium for magical visions and also preserves wedded love.

Amethyst can produce a knowledge of the future through visions and dreams, but it must be worn during sleep.

Anachitis can be used in divination to call up water spirits. It is well to have synochitis on hand as well, which obliges them to stay while they are questioned; else they may disappear into the water again, or be mischievous.

Lodestone is a flamed ferruginous stone, and it is noted for denouncing or revealing adulterous wives, after this manner: the husband must put a fragment of the stone under his wife's pillow without her knowledge. When she is asleep, if she is faithful to him, she will turn and embrace him warmly. But if she has not been faithful to him, she will suffer terrible dreams which will awaken her, and she will give away her secrets in shrieks of terror.

One of the most celebrated forms of divination is a variation of hyromancy, and is divination by coffee grounds; this is practiced by nearly all modern pythonesses. Using a white unglazed plate, they pour some dregs of coffee onto it, allow them to settle, and then carefully drain off the water or liquid. The coffee grounds left on the plate will have formed various patterns, and from these one can see into the future according to their interpretation. Circles indicate money and predict wealth. The number of circles and their size will indicate the extent of this wealth. The shape of a crown indicates success of other sorts, especially State success. The diamond pattern is an omen of success or good fortune in matters of love. Sometimes a number will be discerned, and if this occurs, the individual must not fail to rely upon this number in any impending lottery or contest, for it cannot fail to win for him. Before this reading takes place, though, there are certain ritual incantations which must be said. Often a sorcerer will neglect these prayers and will be surprised that his readings are not accurate, but without them they scarcely can be. So, when adding the water to the ground coffee in the pot, say over it, "Aqua boraxit vemias carajos"; when the mixture is afterward stirred with a spoon, say, "Fixatur et patricam explinabit tornare"; and when pouring the dregs onto the plate, be careful to say, "Hax verticaline, pax Fantas morobum, max destinatus, veida porol." These words are in the language of demons.

Whoever wears emerald in a gold setting will have prophetic dreams.

Electrum or metallic electrum (an alloy of gold and silver), when made into a cup, has magical properties, the foremost of which is that of revealing poison. This is done by the displaying of certain semicircles like rainbows in the liquid, which at the same time hisses and sparkles as if on fire.

Cleidomancy is performed in this way: Suspend a key by a thread from a nail of a virgin's third finger, meanwhile repeating this verse from the Psalms: "Exurge, Domine, adjuva nos, et redime nos propter nomen sanctum tuum." (Arise, O Lord, help us and deliver us for thy holy Name's sake.) If the thing asked can be affirmed, the key will start to revolve, but if it cannot, it will remain stationary.

This is how to detect the identity of a thief: Light a blessed candle and bring it near a mirror or near a pot that has been filled with holy water. A virgin must pronounce these words over it: "Angelo bianco, Angelo santo, per la tua santita e per la mia virginita, mostrami che ha tolto questa cosa." (White angel, holy angel, by thy holiness and by my virginity show me who has stolen this thing.) Whereupon the image of the thief will appear in the mirror or on the surface of the water and can be clearly discerned.

Artephius foresaw events with vases in this manner: By the earthenware vase the past is known, by the copper vase the present is known, and by the glass vase the future is known. In yet another manner, a silver vase filled with wine is set in place of the earthenware one; the copper vase is filled with oil and the glass vase with water. In this manner you can see things present in the earthen vase, things past in the copper, and things future in the silver. These must be shielded from the sun. The weather must be quite calm, and this must have been so for three days or more. You shall work in sunny weather by day and by moonlight at night, and by the light of the stars. Do this in some place distant from noise and distraction, for all must be in silence. You shall be garbed in white and your head and face must be covered with a piece of red silk or fine linen so that nothing is seen but the eyes themselves. In the water the shadow of the thing will be seen; in the oil is seen the appearance of the person; and in the wine is seen the very thing itself. And that is all of it.

Divination by sieve is to find a guilty person. Suspend the sieve by tongs or forceps which can be supported by the midfingers of two assistants. This will be aided by the *daemon urgente,* in order to find who has committed some crime or inflicted some harm. Use this conjuration, the words of which cannot be translated: "Dies, Mies, Jeschet, Bendoefet, Dowima, and Enitemaus." These when uttered compel the daemon to turn the sieve when the culprit is named, and by the turning of the sieve is the culprit made unmistakably known.

Let fall a drop of oil into water and in this way see future things as though in a mirror.

Pour oil onto a mirror and have a virgin gaze therein, as though through a window, and she will see events of the future.

Divination is possible by means of the caul, which is the membrane that sometimes envelops the head of a child at birth. From inspection of this a wise woman can predict the kind of future in store for the child. If it is red, happy days are ahead; but if it is lead-colored, the child will have misfortunes.

If you will take two nuts of any kind and place them on the fire, naming one of them with your own name and the other with the name of your beloved, you shall be given an omen. If they burn away quietly together, your love affair will prosper. But if one moves away from the other, the results will be less fortunate.

To sow the hemp seed: Go out alone about midnight and sow a handful of the seed, repeating as you do so this rhyme:
"Hemp seed, I sow thee, Hemp seed, I sow thee;
And he that is my true love, come behind and harrow me."
Then look over your left shoulder. You will see your true love in the act of harrowing.

The charm of winnowing corn must be gone through in solitude. Take yourself to the barn, but be careful to keep both doors open, or remove them if possible, else the being that appears might close them upon you and then do you harm. Take the instrument that is used for winnowing corn and go through the motions of letting it down against the wind. Do this three times in succession, and the image of your future partner will be seen passing in at one door and out at the other. Sometimes a coffin will appear, followed by mourners, and these may pursue the person about the barn. This is a sign that he will die young.

Here is how to measure the beanstack: Go to the beanstack and go around it three times with arms outstretched as though measuring it. On the third time you will clasp the spirit of your future partner.

Eating the herring is an infallible means of divining the identity of your future beloved. Just before going to bed, eat salt herring, raw or roasted. While you dream, your future husband or wife will appear and bring you a drink of water to quench your thirst.

Dipping the shirt sleeve: Take yourself alone to a stream where the lands of three lairds meet, and there dip into the water the left sleeve of a shirt. Speak not a word or the spell will be ruined. Put the sleeve to dry before the bedroom fire and go to bed, but remain awake. Your future partner will be seen to enter and turn the sleeve so that the other side will dry as well.

Take three plates and put them in a row upon the table. Put clean water in one of these, foul water in a second, and let the third remain empty. The one who wants to know his future should be blindfolded and brought up to the table. Let him put forward his left hand. If it touches the clean water, then the future mate will be young and handsome and a bachelor or a maid. But if it touches the foul, this signs that it will be a widower or a widow. If it touch the empty dish, the person will be blessed with a single life. Repeat this ceremony three times, arranging the plates differently each time.

Go forth alone at night, to the nearest lime kiln. Throw into it a clue of blue yarn, which you will then wind off on to a fresh clue. As the end nears, you will feel someone take hold of the thread still in the kiln. Ask aloud, "Who holds this thread?" And from beneath a voice will utter the name of your future partner.

Alphitomancy will prove the guilt or innocence of a suspected person: If many are accused and it is desired to find out the true culprit, take a loaf of barley and give a portion to each person suspected. Those who are innocent will suffer no ill effects, but the guilty one will suffer an attack of indigestion. Some say that each of the persons, just before eating, should say, "If I am deceiving you may this bread act upon me foul." There is another way this can be done, such as to learn if one's mate is faithful. Take a quantity of pure barley flour and knead it with milk and some salt, but add no leavening. Roll it up in greased paper and cook it among the cinders. Then take it out and rub it with verbena leaves and give it to one whom you suspect of deceit. If the suspicion is justified, that person will be unable to digest it.

Go to a clean cell where there is no light and dig a new hole in an east wall. Take a white lamp in which no trace of gum water has been, and with clean wick, and fill it up with genuine oasis oil, then

84

recite the spells-of-praising-Ra-at-dawn-in-his-rising. Bring the lamp after lighting to a place opposite the sun and recite the spells four times and take it into the cell, being pure yourself, and take a boy as well, and say the spells to the boy. He will not look at the lamp but will keep his eyes closed. Say the spells seven times. Put pure frankincense on the brazier and put your finger on his head. Then make him open his eyes in the direction of the lamp. He will see the shadow of the god, and he can ask that which you desire to know. This must be done at midday in a place without light. If you are asking for a spirit damned, put in the lamp a wick of sail cloth and fill it with clean butter. If it is other, put pure genuine oil in the lamp and a clean wick. If you bring a woman to a man, use ointment of roses in the lamp. Lay the lamp on a new brick and the boy should sit on another brick. Cry down into his head five times.

CHAPTER FIVE

Dealing with Demons

A cock is lucky and should go into a new house first. But he may become the victim of demons; if he upsets a dish, this is what has happened, and he must be killed promptly before he infects the house.

Abyssum is an herb used in exorcising a haunted house. One has to sign it with the sign of the cross and hang it up at the four corners of the house.

If you want to raise the Devil, make a circle, put an old hat in the center of it, and then repeat aloud the Lord's Prayer, backwards.

Pontica is a stone, blue with red stars or veins, like blood. It compels the Devil to answer questions put to him, and then sends him away.

Lights, especially candles, burn blue if there are apparitions or spirits present, which is probably due to the sulphurous atmosphere accompanying such specters.

The common willow tree, as most people know, is under the Devil's protection. This is why, if one casts a knot upon a young willow and sits under it and then renounces his baptism, the Devil will at once confer upon him supernatural powers.

A witch may be punished in this way: Have some of the milk of a dried-up cow. Set it in a pot to boil, and strike thereon with a stick. The Devil will at the same time deal blows to the witch, and this will force her to come and take off the spell.

The gypsies tell of an evil spirit called the chagrin or cagrino: It is similar to a hedgehog in appearance, yellow in color, a foot and a half in length and a span in breadth. The chagrin preys on horses especially and rides them into a state of exhaustion. The following day they appear sick and worn out, with tangled manes, and they will have sweated profusely. This is what to do. Tether the horses to a stake which has been rubbed with garlic juice. Lay a red thread on the ground in the form of a cross; or mix some of the hair of the animals with salt, meal, and the blood of a bat, cook a bread of this, and smear the hoof of the horse with it. Take the empty vessel which contained the mixture and put it in the trunk of a high tree while uttering this spell:
> Tarry, pipkin, in this tree,
> Till such time as full ye be.

Disenchant an animal by sprinkling salt in a porringer with some of the blood of the bewitched animal and saying prayers for nine days.

If a woman wishes to become a sorceress, she must sacrifice a live cock on a termite nest, cutting the bird in half from head to tail and placing it on an altar in front of which she must dance and sing until the two pieces come together again and the bird regains its life and crows.

A Spanish chant is used to stop rain by fooling the witch who has raised it into thinking one doesn't mind the rain, and at the same time belittling her importance:

> Que llueva, que llueva
> La vieja esta en la cueva
> Los pajaritos cantan
> Y la luna se levanta.

> (How it's raining, how it's raining.
> The old woman is in her lair
> The little birds sing
> And the moon rises.)

Elder trees are witch-prone; often witches use them for homes. They should be avoided for this reason. Never make a child's bed out of elder. Do not burn elder branches in a fire, as this may provoke the witch and may also release evil spells which she has stored in the wood. If it is necessary to cut down an elder tree or trim it, one must apologize beforehand to the witch of that tree and make this promise: "When I am a tree you can have some of my wood in return." If the woodsman does not apologize, he will suffer some injury while he cuts the tree.

Take a shining piece of steel and smear it over with the juice of a mugwort, and make it to fume; it will cause invoked spirits to appear.

The Hand of Glory is prepared in the following manner: A murderer swinging from the gallows must have his hand severed at the wrist. This is mummified in a brine of salt, black pepper, and brimstone; a kind of wick is plaited from the hair of the dead man steeped in fat and sesame. A candle is formed. When these wicks are lighted a deep sleep falls over all who are in the house and they cannot be raised.

An invocation to bind spirits to the will: "I adjure and command you, ye strong, mighty, and most powerful spirits, who are rulers of this day and hour, that ye obey me in this my cause by (here you state your case or what it is you desire, such as making all my enemies bow down before me and apologize for misdeeds to me) and I bind you by the name of Almighty God, and by our Lord Jesus Christ, and by his Precious Blood, and on pain of everlasting damnation, that you labor for this and complete and accomplish the whole of this my will and desire, and not depart until the whole of this my will and desire be fulfilled, and when you have accomplished the whole of these my commands you shall be released from all these bonds and demands, and this I guarantee through the blood of the Redeemer and on pain of my future happiness. Let all Angels praise the Lord. Amen."

To relieve the spell of a witch she must be scratched by the victim until blood is drawn.

Werewolves can be killed with silver bullets, especially silver that has been consecrated in church. Also, if a werewolf abstains from human flesh for nine years, he will revert to human form.

Certain points are most especially important when making a magic circle: The Four Divine Names must necessarily be inscribed therein with four crosses interposed. It is essential that the circle be sacred and hallowed in the Name of the Holy, Blessed, and Glorious Trinity. For the ritual benediction, one must say: "We consecrate this piece of ground for our defense, so that no spirit whatsoever shall be able to break these boundaries, neither be able to cause injury nor detriment to any of us here assembled; but that they be compelled to stand before this circle, and answer truly our demands." Evil spirits will attempt every sort of cunning to lure someone from the circle, but those within must remember never to put a foot beyond its protective boundaries. The spirits must first be licensed to depart, and this is necessary even though no spirits have appeared, for although they are not visible they may yet be present. As to other points, the magician must have various instruments—the pentacle, the rod, the lamens. He should wear a garment of white linen, a kind of alb, and be girt about the loins with a girdle. Wax lights which have been consecrated should be burning the while. There should be suffumigations of frankincense.

One wishing to raise demons or spirits must go to some lonely and deserted place, as for example the depths of a wood, or a subterraneous cavern, or some distant moor where several roads meet, or to a deserted abbey or the ruins of an ancient castle; some go to the seashore, and others to a private churchyard. It should be a solemn place, and melancholy. Go there between midnight and one o'clock when the moon is full, or else when thunder rolls and lightning flashes, for this is a comfortable season for spirits. The sorcerer should wear a robe, or *de pontificalibus*, an ephod of white linen over a priestly robe of black bombazine, and all of this girt with a consecrated girdle. He should wear a high crowned hat of sable silk. His priestly shoes should be written over with the name Tetragrammaton or the word of four letters, the Hebrew YHWH or JHVH. Summon the spirit by the blood of Abel, by Seth's righteousness, by the prayers of Noah, and by the voice of thunder and by the day of dread judgment. Perfumes are necessary, frankincense being a good one. Sacrifices of blood are required for some spirits, and will not be a hindrance in any case. The sorcerer must never forget the necessity of discharging the familiar at the end of the ceremony and bidding him go. If it is the spirit of a suicide one wishes to conjure he will need a consecrated torch bound with St. John's wort. He should have at hand a chafing dish in which is kept a fire made of charcoal and fed with wine, mastic, and gum aromatic. Have at hand a measure of sweet oil which will nourish the flames; when the spirit is raised, use the oil to produce the brightest flame. As to the fumigations, these vary. One can be concocted with spicery, bdellium (a gum resin similar to myrhh), euphorbium (a very acrid gum resin derived from a Moroccan spurge), lodestone, both black and white hellebore, and sulphur, all this made into amalgama with blood from a black cat and blood from a man.

Exorcism formula: "I adjure thee, O serpent of old, by the Judge of the living and the dead, by the Creator of the world Who hath power to cast into

Hell, that thou depart forthwith from this house. He that commands thee, accursed demon, is He that commanded the winds and the sea and the storm. He that commands thee is He that ordered thee to be hurled down from the height of Heaven into the lower parts of the earth. He that commands thee is He that bade thee depart from Him. Hearken, then, Satan, and fear. Get thee gone, vanquished and cowed, when thou art bidden in the name of our Lord Jesus Christ, Who will come to judge the living and the dead and all the world by fire. Amen."

Anyone who sleeps overnight in the open on a Friday under a full moon will become a werewolf.

In Italy, it is believed that anyone conceived at the time of the new moon will become a werewolf.

Drinking water from a wolf's footprint, drinking from a stream where a wolfpack drank, or eating a wolf's brains are all certain methods of becoming a werewolf.

There are two ways of finding a vampire's grave. In the first, one drives a white stallion through the cemetery. It must be a horse who has never gone to stud and who has never stumbled. He will refuse to step over the grave of the vampire. In the second method, a black stallion is used, one that is sure-footed and virginal, and he must be ridden by a virginal boy. Again they will be unable to pass over the grave of this odious creature.

To exorcise demons: Drop salt into holy water so as to form the shape of a cross. Then make the sign of the cross over the water, and afterward offer it up for God's blessing before sprinkling it on the forehead of a woman who had been conscious of the evil presence. Then banish the spirit from the four corners of the room. When this is done, pour the water on the ground.

The following is a Chaldean conjuration of the Maskim, seven terrible spirits of the abyss, of whom Mephistopheles is one:
    A charm of awful power
    A spell that's older than the walls, long buried,
    Of Babylon; ere Nineveh was dreamed;
    Was old beyond the power of computation.
    They are Seven, they are Seven . . . Seven they
      are:
    They sit by the way. They sleep in the deep:
    Down far . . .
    Seven they are!
    They are Seven, they are Seven . . . Seven are
      they!
    Out of the Abyss they rise, when day
    Sinks into darkness.
    Seven are they!
    Born in the bowels o' the hills,
    Evil ones, sowers of ills:
    Setters of unseen snares,
    Deaf to all pity, all prayers:
    Male they are not,
    Female they are not,
    No wives have they known,
    No children begot.
    The Fiends, they are Seven:
    Disturbers of Heaven;
    They are Seven, they are Seven . . . Seven they
      are!

This is a concoction to cause demoniacal posses-sion: It is made from sacred hosts and consecrated wine, with powdered goat, human bones, skulls of children, hair, nails, flesh, and wizard's semen, with bits of goose, female rat, and brains.

Deadly ointments of evil properties can be made by these receipts: Hemlock, juice of the aconite plant, poplar leaves, and soot; or take water hemlock, sweet flag, cinquefoil, bat's blood, belladonna, and oil; or make one with baby's fat, juice of water hemlock, aconite, cinquefoil, belladonna, and soot.

A pact with the Devil:
1. Lucifer, you are bound to deliver to me immedi-ately 100,000 pounds of gold!
2. You will deliver to me the first Tuesday of every month 1,000 pounds of money in gold.
3. You will bring me this gold in current money, of such kind that not only I but also all those to whom I may wish to give some may use it.
4. The aforesaid gold must not be false, must not disappear in one's hand, or turn to stone or coals. It should be metal stamped by the hands of men, legal and valid in all lands.
5. If I need a considerable sum of money, no mat-ter when or for what purpose, you are duty-bound to deliver to me secret or buried treasure. Nor need I fetch it myself from wherever it may be hidden or buried, but you must deliver it into my hands with-out any trouble to me, to wherever I happen to be at the time, to dispose of according to my own wishes and pleasure.
6. You are bound to cause no injury to my body and limbs, and do nothing to weaken my health, but

preserve me from human illnesses and injury for fifty years.

7. If, contrary to our expectations, I should happen to become ill, you are bound to procure for me proved remedies to help me regain my previous good health as soon as possible.

8. Our agreement is to begin on this date in the year ———, and to end on the same day in ———. You are not to tamper with this period or encroach on my rights or make a false reckoning (as you have often formerly been accustomed to do).

9. When my time has finally run out, you are to let me die like all other men, without shame or disgrace, and be honorably buried.

10. You are bound to make me loved and accepted by the King and all aristocrats, by high and low, men and women, so that I may always be assured of good will and affection, and that everybody will grant without question what I may desire of them.

11. You are bound to transport me (and any other) without injury to the ends of the world, wherever I desire, no matter how far distant. You are to make me immediately so expert in the language of that place that I shall be able to speak it fluently. When I have satisfied my curiosity sufficiently, you will bring me back again, uninjured, to my home.

12. You are bound to protect me from all harm from bombs, firearms, and other weapons, so that nothing may strike me and injure my body or limbs.

13. You are bound to assist me in my dealings with the King and help me prevail over my special enemies.

14. You are bound to provide me with a magic ring, so that whenever I put it on my finger I shall become invisible and invulnerable.

15. You are bound to give me true and thorough information, without distortion or ambiguity, about any question I ask of you.

16. You are bound to give me advance warning of any secret plot against me, and to give me ways and means to thwart those plots and to bring them to naught.

17. You are bound to teach me whatever languages I may desire to learn, so that I can read, converse, and express opinions in them as perfectly as if I had known them thoroughly from childhood.

18. You are bound to endow me with good sense, understanding, and intelligence, so that I can discuss all problems logically and can give an informed opinion about them.

19. You are bound to protect and look after me in all courts of justice and council chambers of King, Bishop, or Pope, before whom I might be summoned.

20. You are bound to protect me and my household from injury, whether domestic or foreign, from theft, and from harm.

21. I am to be permitted to lead my life in outward appearance like a good Christian, and to attend divine service without your interfering.

22. You are bound to teach me how to prepare medical prescriptions and the correct use and administering of them in dosage and weight.

23. If on any occasion, skirmish, or fight I should be attacked and set upon, you are to take up the challenge for me and produce help and assistance against all enemies.

24. You are bound to prevent anyone, no matter whom, from knowing about our accord and compact.

25. As often as I desire your presence, you are to appear to me in a loving and agreeable form, never in a frightening or horrible shape.

26. You are to see that each and every person shall do my bidding.

27. You are to promise me and bind yourself to keep unbroken these clauses, individually and collectively, and to comply assiduously with all of them. If you fail me in the slightest degree and display any negligence, then this pact and accord is null and void and of no force whatever.

28. In return for the foregoing promises, I swear and vow to deliver into your power several men and women. Furthermore, I renounce God, the most Holy Trinity; I wholly renounce the vows made for me at baptism. I step forward with you in a new alliance and submit myself to you both in body and soul, forever into eternity.

If one wishes to destroy a vampire, it is necessary to drive a wooden stake through his heart. He will emit a terrifying shriek, blood will rush forth, and the body will at once begin to decompose. It is necessary, however, that the stake should be of hawthorne or whitethorn, and it must be driven with one blow only. Cut off the head with a sexton's spade. The head, body, stake, and coffin must then all be burned.

This is the pact signed between the Devils and Father Grandier, the first example being the pact, written from right to left, with words spelled backwards and using the conventional Latin contractions, followed by the same declaration in conventional Latin and then the English translation. After this is the Pact of Allegiance signed by Grandier, and its English translation:

Pact between the Devils and Grandier
mlE ntvL bbzlB ntS etnvuj rfcL snetpp soN tcap tpecca smebah eidh qsila toratsA qta ciuh te .e sibon iuq rdnarG brU siredeof munigriv merolf lum meroma mecillop oudirt bacinrof .po te pulov noh nom suced ona ni lemes terffo sboN .re arac illi teirbe sbon te ealccE as baclucoc sdep bus gis gas silef giv na teviv tcap q : ture suispi tagor .D delam son tni aetsop nev te moh art ni
mead ssoc tni fni ni tcaF
(Signatures of the demons)
rfcL bubezleB sanataS
nahtaiveL imilE
htoratsA
mod pcnirp mead te baid gam sop giS
tprcs htrblB

In conventional Latin:
Nos praepotens Lucifer, juvante Satan, Belzebub, Leviathan, Elimi, atque Astaroth, aliisque, hodie habemus acceptum pactum foederis Urbani Granderi qui nobis est. Et huic pollicemur amorem mulierum, florem virginim, decus monacharum, honores, voluptates et opes. Fornicabitur triduo; ebrietas illi cara erit. Nobis offeret semel in anno sanguinis sigillum, sub pedibus conculcabit sacra ecclesiae et nobis rogationes ipsius erunt; quo pacto vivet annos viginti felix in terra hominum, et veniet postea inter nos maleficere Deo.
Factum in infernis, inter consilia daemonum
(Signatures of the demons)
Sigilla posuere magister diabolus et daemones

principes domini
Baalberith scriptor.

English translation:
We, the all-powerful Lucifer, seconded by Satan,
Beelzebub, Leviathan, Elimi, Astaroth, and others,
have today accepted the pact of alliance with
Urbain Grandier, who is on our side. And we
promise him the love of women, the flower of vir-
gins, the chastity of nuns, worldly honors, pleas-
ures, and riches. He will fornicate every three
days; intoxication will be dear to him. He will offer to us once a year a tribute marked with his
blood; he will trample under foot the sacraments
of the Church, and he will say his prayers to us.
By virtue of this pact, he will live happily for
twenty years on earth among men, and finally
will come among us to curse God. Done in Hell, in
the council of the Devils.
(Signatures of the demons) Satan, Beelzebub,
Lucifer, Elimi, Leviathan, Astaroth.
Notarized the signature and mark of the Chief
Devil, and my lords the Princes of Hell. Counter-
signed, Baalberith, recorder.

Pact of Alliance as signed by Grandier:
Domine magisterque Lucifer te deum et prin-
cipem agnosco, et polliceor tibi servire et obedire
quandiu potero vivere. Et renuncio alterum Deum
et Jesum Christum et alios sanctos atque sanctas
et Ecclesiam Apostolicam et Romanam et omnia
ipsius scramenta et omnes orationes et rogationes
quibus fideles possint intercedere pro me; et tibi
polliceor quid faciam quotquot malum potero, et
attrahere ad mala per omnes; et abrenuncio
chrismam et baptismum, et omnia merita Jesu

Christi et ipsius sanctorum; et si deero tuae servi-
tui et adorationi; et si non oblationem mei ipsius
fecero, ter quoque die, tibi do vitam meam sicut
tuam. Feci hoc anno et die.
  Urb. Grandier. Extractum ex infernis.

English translation:
  My lord and master Lucifer, I acknowledge thee
  as my God and Prince, and promise to serve and
  obey thee as long as I shall live. And I renounce
  the other God, as well as Jesus Christ, all the
  saints, the apostolic and Roman Church, all the
  sacraments, and all the prayers and petitions by
  which the faithful might intercede for me. And
  I promise thee that I will do as much evil as I can,
  and that I will draw everyone else to evil. I renounce chrism, baptism, all the merits of Jesus
  Christ and his saints. And if I fail to serve and
  adore thee, and if I do not pay thee homage thrice
  every day, I give you my life as thine own. Made
  this year and day.
    Urbain Grandier. Extracted from hell.

*This is the customary practice for determining
whether one who is sick is actually possessed by a
demon:* Priests must secretly apply to the sick man
a writing with the sacred words of God, or some
relic of the saint, or a blessed waxen Agnus Dei, or
some holy thing. A priest must place his hand and
his stole upon the head of the patient and pronounce sacred words. Then the sick person will
begin to shake and tremble with fright and make
convulsive and confused movements, and say confused things. If there is a devil lodging in his head,
the patient will feel dreadful pains there, or his face
may become flushed as though afire. Sometimes the

100

demon will be in his eyes, and if this is the case these will roll about wildly. If the demon is in his back his limbs will convulse and sometimes the body may become as rigid as steel, so that force cannot bend it. At other times the possessed person will fall down as if dead, but the priest can command them to arise and they will do so. They may appear to be strangling, and this is because the demon is in their throats. If he is lodged in or about the heart or the lungs there will be panting and palpitations, but if the spirit is in the stomach he will cause hiccoughs or vomiting, or the patient will be unable to take food, or to retain it. The demon may cause them to pass something like a little ball from the anus, usually with roaring and crying. Wind may grip them in the abdomen, and there may be certain fumes of sulphur or other strong smells.

There is an ointment which witches use for going to the Sabbat, even though their corporeal selves may seem to remain in the same place. The fat of child is the principal ingredient, to which is added juice of water parsnip, aconite, cinquefoil, deadly nightshade, and soot.

Bay branches in the house, if green, will prevent a poltergeist from working mischief.

Certain herbs are effective in driving away demons, as are stones and other materials. The castor oil plant and the coral stone are powerful, as are jet and jasper and menstrual blood. The following is an incense against the incubus: sweet flag, cubeb seed, roots of aristolochia (a large genus of mostly tropical herbs), great and small cardamon, ginger, long pepper, clove pink, cinnamon, cloves, mace, nutmegs, resin, benzoin, aloe wood and root, and fragrant sandal. Brew these in three and a half quarts of brandy and water.

Red thread and rowan wood, tied inside a person's garments, will prevent bewitchment.

The order of Exorcism from the Rituale Romanum set forth by order of the Supreme Pontiff, Paul V (the sign of the cross must be made where * is seen): The priest, robed in surplice and violet stole, one end of which is placed round the neck of the possessed individual, who must be bound if he is violent, sprinkles all present with holy water, after which the service begins and follows this schedule:
1. The Litany.
2. Psalm 54 ("Save me, O God, by thy name").
3. Adjuration imploring God's grace for the proposed exorcism against the wicked dragon and a caution to the possessing spirit to tell his name, and the day and the hour of his going out, by some sign.
4. The Gospel, John 1 and/or Mark 16; Luke 11.
5. Preparatory prayers. Here the priest, while protecting himself and the possessed with the sign of the cross, places part of his stole about the neck of the possessed and his right hand on the patient's head, and says the following with great resolution and faith.
6. First exorcism: "I exorcize thee, most vile spirit, the very embodiment of our enemy, the entire specter, the whole legion, in the name of Jesus Christ, to * get out and flee from the creature of God * *.
"He himself commands thee Who has ordered

102

those cast down from the heights of heaven to the depths of the earth. He commands thee, He Who commanded the sea, the winds, and the tempests.

"Hear therefore and fear, O Satan, enemy of the faith, foe to the human race, producer of death, thief of life, destroyer of justice, root of evils, kindler of vices, seducer of men, betrayer of nations, inciter of envy, origin of avarice, cause of discord, procurer of sorrows. Why dost thou stand and resist, when thou knowest that Christ the Lord will destroy thy strength? Fear Him Who was immolated in Isaac, sold in Joseph, slain in the Lamb, crucified in man, and then was triumphant over Hell. (The following signs of the cross should be made on the forehead of the possessed)

"Depart therefore in the name of the * Father, and of the * Son, and of the Holy * Ghost; give place to the Holy Ghost, by the sign of the * Cross of Jesus Christ our Lord, Who with the Father and the same Holy Ghost liveth and reigneth one God, forever and ever, world without end."

7. Prayer for success and continued signs of the cross over the victim.

8. Second exorcism: "I adjure thee, thou old serpent, by the Judge of the quick and the dead, by thy maker and the maker of the world, by Him Who has power to send thee to hell, that thou depart quickly from this servant of God (name of victim), who returns to the bosom of the Church, with fear and the affliction of thy terror. I adjure thee again (* on his forehead), not in my infirmity, but by the virtue of the Holy Ghost, that thou depart from this servant of God, (name), whom Almighty God hath made in His own image.

"Yield, therefore; yield not to me, but to the minister of Christ. For His power urges thee, Who subjugated thee to His cross. Tremble at His arm, Who led the soul to light after the lamentations of Hell had been subdued. May the body of man be a terror to thee (* on his chest), let the image of God be terrible to thee (* on his forehead). Resist not, neither delay to flee from this man, since it has pleased Christ to dwell in this body. And although thou knowest me to be none the less a sinner, do not think me contemptible.

"For it is God who commands thee *.

"The majesty of Christ commands thee *.

"God the Father commands thee *.

"God the Son commands thee *.

"God the Holy Ghost commands thee *.

"The sacred cross commands thee *.

"The faith of the holy apostles Peter and Paul and of all other saints commands thee *.

"The blood of the martyrs commands thee *.

"The constancy of the confessors commands thee *.

"The devout intercession of all saints commands thee *.

"The virtue of the mysteries of the Christian faith commands thee *.

"Go out, therefore, thou transgressor. Go out, thou seducer, full of deceit and guile, enemy of virtue, persecutor of innocence. O most dire one, give place; give place, thou most impious; give place to Christ, in Whom thou hast found nothing of thy words, Who hath despoiled thee, Who hath led thee captive and hath plundered thy goods, Who hath cast thee into outer darkness, where for thee and thy ministers is prepared annihilation.

"But why, truculent one, dost thou withstand? Why, rash creature, dost thou refuse?

"Thou art accursed by Almighty God, Whose statutes thou hast transgressed.

"Thou art accused by His son, Jesus Christ, our Lord, Whom thou didst dare to tempt and presume to crucify.

"Thou art accused by the human race, to whom by thy persuasion thou hast given to drink the poison of death.

"Therefore I adjure thee, most wicked dragon, *draco nequissime,* in the name of the * immaculate Lamb, Who trod upon the asp and basilisk, Who trampled the lion and dragon, to depart from this man (* let the sign be made upon the forehead), to depart from the Church of God (* let the sign be made on those standing by). Tremble and flee at the invocation of the name of that Lord at Whom Hell trembles, to Whom the virtues of Heaven, the powers of dominions are subject, Whom cherubim and seraphim with unwearied voices praise, saying, Holy, holy, holy, Lord God of Saboath.

"The Word made flesh * commands thee.

"He Who was born of the Virgin * commands thee.

"Jesus of Nazareth commands thee, Who, although thou didst despise His disciples, bade thee go, crushed and prostrate, out of the man, and in His presence, when He had separated thee from the man, thou didst presume to go into a herd of swine.

"Therefore, adjured now in His * name, depart from this man, whom He has created. It is hard for thee to wish to resist. It is hard for thee to kick against the pricks *. Because the more slowly thou

105

go out, the more the punishment against thee increases, since thou despisest not men but Him Who is Lord of the quick and dead, Who shall come to judge the quick and the dead and the world by fire."
9. Prayer.
10. Third and final exorcism: "Therefore, I adjure thee, most vile spirit, the entire specter, the very embodiment of Satan, in the name of Jesus Christ * of Nazareth, Who, after His baptism in Jordan, was led into the wilderness and overcame thee in thine own habitations, that thou stop assaulting him whom He hath formed from the dust of the earth to the honor of His glory, and that thou tremble not at the human weakness in miserable man but at the image of Almighty God.

"Therefore yield to God, Who by his servant Moses drowned thee and thy malice in Pharoah and in his army in the abyss.

"Yield to God, Who made thee flee when expelled from King Saul with spiritual songs through His most faithful servant, David.

"Yield to God, * Who condemned thee in Judas Iscariot the traitor.

"For He beats thee with divine * scourges, in Whose sight, trembling and crying out with thy legions, thou hast said, What art Thou to us, O Jesus, Son of the most high God? Art thou come hither to torture us before our time? He presses on thee with perpetual flames, Who shall say at the end of time to the wicked: Depart from me, you cursed, into everlasting fire, which is prepared for the devil and his angels.

"For thee, impious one, and for thy angels are prepared words which never die.

"For thee and thy angels is prepared the un-

106

quenchable fire; because thou art the chief of accursed murder, thou art the author of incest, the head of sacrilege, the master of the worst actions, the teacher of heretics, the inventor of all obscenities. Therefore, O impious one, go out. Go out, thou scoundrel, go out with all thy deceits, because God has willed that man be His temple.

"But why dost thou delay longer here? Give honor to God, the Father Almighty, to Whom every knee is bent.

"Give place to the Lord Jesus Christ, * Who shed for man His most Precious blood.

"Give place to the Holy Ghost, Who through His blessed apostle Peter manifestly struck thee in Simon Magus, Who condemned thy deceit in Ananias and Sapphira, Who smote thee in Herod the King because he did not give God honor, Who through His apostle Paul destroyed thee in the magician Elymas by the mist of blindness, and through the same apostle by His word of command bade thee come out of the pythoness.

"Now therefore depart. * Depart, thou seducer. Thy abode is the wilderness, thy habitation is the serpent. Be humbled and prostrate. Now there is no time to delay. For behold, the Lord God approaches quickly, and His fire will glow before Him and precede Him and burn up His enemies on every side. For if thou hast deceived man, thou canst not mock God.

"He expels thee from Whose eye nothing is secret.

"He expels thee to Whose power all things are subject.

"He excludes thee Who has prepared for thee and thy angels everlasting Hell; out of Whose mouth

the sharp sword will go, He Who shall come to judge the quick and the dead and the world by fire."
11. Final prayers, including canticles, creed, and various psalms. In addition, fumigation and flagellation can be employed.

An Egyptian invocation:
    O oualbpaga!
    O Kammara!
    O Kamalo!
    O Karhenmon!
    O Amagaaa!
(These are magically transfigured names of the gods Osiris and Seth.)

A Chaldean incantation:
    He who forges the image, he who enchants—
    The spiteful face, the evil eye,
    The mischievous mouth, the mischievous tongue,
    The mischievous lips, the mischievous words,
    Spirit of the Sky, remember!
    Spirit of the Earth, remember!

A Kabbalist formula for invoking demons: AGLA (This is made from the initial letters of the expression Aieth Gadol Leolam Adonai; God will be great forever)

A Kabbalist talisman against sickness: (to be inscribed upon parchment)
    Ananisapta

A formula for invoking evil demons:
    Xilka, Xilka, Besa, Besa

An incantation to banish demons:
          Ochnotinos
           Chnotinos
             Notinos
               Tinos
                Inos
                  Nos
                    Os

A spell to banish demons:
    Lofaham,
    Solomon,
    Iyouel,
    Iyosenaoui.

CHAPTER SIX

To Alter the Form

In the annals of witchcraft, it is common for the caster of spells to change from one living form to another. The word "familiar" sometimes means the witch in another, but still human, form. In the practice of witchcraft a "familiar" is really an animal that serves in a domestic capacity. It need not always be an animal—a familiar can take on any form, even an inanimate one.

The vampire is a common enough figure in witchcraft. It is a witch who disguises himself or herself in the body of a bat in order to travel undetected from point to point. A seasoned witch can change form at will, and the methods of doing so are varied and interesting.

The secret of invisibility: Sorcerers were quick to master ways of rendering themselves invisible. Armed with this knowledge, they could venture into gatherings or enter houses without anyone becoming suspicious of their presence. No doubt many of you will be eager to know the secret; here are several to choose from, all endorsed by notable experts:

Chant the following prayer for one hour without interruption: "Athal, Bathel, Nothe, Jhoram, Asey, Cleyungit, Gabellin, Semeney, Mencheno, Bal, Lebenenten, Palcin, Timgimiel, Plegas, Peneme, Gruora, Hean, Ha, Ararna, Avira, Ayla, Seye, Permies, Seney, Levesso, Huay, Baruchalu, Acuth, Tural, Buchard, Caratim, Per misericordiam abibit ergo mortale perficiat qua hoc opus ut invisibiliter ire possim."

It is written that at this point, if it is considered opportune, certain characters may be written in bat's blood and a conjuration may be performed, but this is quite discretionary; the essential thing is to continue the prayer thus: "O to Pontation, Magister invisibilitatis cum Magistris tuis, Tenem, Musach, Motagren, Bries verl Brys, Domedis, Ugemal, Abdita, Patribisisb, Tangadentet, Ciclap, Clinet, Z, Succentat, Colleig, Bereith et Plintia, Gastaril, Oletel, conjuro te Pontation, et ipsos Ministros invisibilitatis per illum qui contremere facit orbem per Coelum et terram, Cherubim et Seraphim et per illum qui generare fecit in virgine et Deus est cum homine, ut hoc experimentum perfectae perficiam, est in quaecumquae hora voluero, sim invisibilis; Iterum conjuro te et tuos Ministros, pro Stabuches et Machaerom, Esay, Enitgiga, Bellis, Semonei, ut Statim venias cum dictis ministris tuis et perficias hoc opus sicut scitis, et hoc experimentum men invisibilem faciat, ut nemo me videat. Amen."

The manuscript rightly adds: "Note that it is absolutely necessary to know the above principles!" It goes without saying that these prayers are not efficacious unless spoken in Latin. A version in the vulgar tongue would have no influence over the occult powers surrounding us. I give a translation of this beautiful conjuration all the same, in case some of my readers should not get the sense of it quite easily: "O thou, Pontation! Master of invisibility, with thy masters (here follow the names of the various masters), I conjure thee, Pontation, and these same masters of invisibility, by Him Who makes the universe tremble, by Heaven and Earth, Cherubim and Seraphim, and by Him Who made the Virgin conceive and Who is God and Man, that I may accomplish this experiment in perfectibility, in such sort that at any hour I desire I may be invisible; again I conjure thee and thy ministers also, by Stabuches and Mechaerom, Esey, Enirigiga, Bellis, and Semonei, that thou come straightway with thy said ministers and that thou perform this work as you all know how, and that this experiment may make me invisible, in such wise that no one may see me. Amen."

It is also recommended, in order to make oneself invisible, to carry the heart of a bat and black hen or a frog under the right arm.

Another method is to wear the Ring of Gyges on your finger. You can thereby become visible or invisible at will, simply by turning the stone inward or outward. This ring must be made of fixed mercury; it must be set with a little stone to be found in a lapwing's nest, and around the stone must be engraved the words, "Jesus passant * par le milieu d'eux * e'en allait." ("Jesus, passing through the midst of them, went his way." Luke 4:30) You must put the ring on your finger, and if you look at yourself in a mirror and cannot see the ring it is a certain sign that it has been successfully manufactured.

To make yourself invisible, simply rub your body with an ointment manufactured from the incinerated bodies of newly born babes. Mix this substance with the blood of four night birds, owls preferably. It is then instructed that the invoker must fast for fifteen days. Then when the fast is ended, drink alcoholic beverages until you are stupefied; drink thusly for five consecutive days. After sundown on the fifth day, you will be able to render yourself invisible or visible simply by concentrating thereon. It is suggested that wine is preferred insofar as the alcoholic beverage is concerned; or, if the invoker so desires, hemp or poppy seeds can be substituted, in which event they should be steeped in the wine.

Seek out the belocolus stone. This is a whitish-colored stone with a black pupil, similar to the human eye. When it is worn on the battlefield, the enemy will not be able to discern you, although your friends will see you plainly.

Seek out any boraginaceous herb or shrub of the genus heliotropium, the wild-growing variety—the flower or plant that turns toward the sun. Pick a goodly bouquet, and reduce half of the quantity to juices. When this is accomplished, rub the juices on the heliotrope plant itself. It will enable the possessor thereof to render himself impervious to poisonous snakes, insects, etc. The solution should be applied to all exposed parts of the anatomy.

Another stone that can be worn to render the wearer invisible is the garatonicus, a reddish-colored stone available in most parts of the world.

Collect fourteen pieces of silken ribbon with red and yellow colors dominating the collection. Add thereto several lengths of yarn and the urine of a large white wolf. Drench the ribbons and yarns in the urine and allow to dry in a grassy knoll. Permit the article privacy for three days, at the end of which time return to the knoll and retrieve your article. Drape around the neck. You will be rendered invisible and will also be endowed with the power to transmit yourself unseen from point to point.

To assume the shape of an animal: If you desire to assume the form of a wild beast, particularly a wolf, you should venture into a lonely forest or to the top of a desolate hill on the night when the moon is full. There in the brightness of the moon you must disrobe, rendering yourself completely naked. Draw a wide circle around you on the ground and stand in the center of that circle for several moments, contemplate the great planets, and concentrate upon the masters of magic. Then draw around you a second circle. The outer circle should measure seven feet in diameter and the smaller inside circle should be approximately three feet across the middle. In the confines of these drawn circles, you must build a fire and carry to it a cauldron, which is placed upon the blazing fire; the waters of the cauldron should be brought to a boil. Place in the boiling water hemlock, opium, henbane, and parsley. When this is accomplished you must utter the following incantation:

"Wolves, vampires, satyrs, ghosts!
Elect of all the devilish hosts!
I pray you send hither,
Send hither, send hither,
The great grey shape that makes men shiver!"

Smear your body with the witch's ointment and gird your waist with the pelt of a wolf. Under the light of the moon, kneel down and remain so until a cloud has passed over the brightness of the moon. Presently, upon the passing of the cloud, a demon will appear to you, and you will be granted the power of metamorphosis by him.

Another means employed to turn a man into a wolf is as follows: Remove your clothing under the light of a full moon. Urinate in a circle drawn on the ground. The moon will turn dark, and you will be turned into the shape of a werewolf.

If you wish to assume the shape of a rabbit: The following incantation must be repeated aloud clearly, three times in succession:

"I shall go into a hare,
With sorrow, and sighing, and little care,
And I shall go in the Devil's name,
Until I come home again."

For all of the above transformations, once the desired shape has been obtained and the practioner desires to return to human form, he merely recites the following:

115

"Here, Here, God send thee care.
I am a (name of animal likeness) now.
But I shall be a woman (or man) soon.
Here, Here, God send thee care."

Another chant is:
"I shall go into a (name of the animal you re-
    semble)
With sorrow and sigh and a black shot
I shall come out of the likeness of the (name of
    animal)
With sorrow and sigh and a black shot
I shall go in the Devil's name.
Ay while I come home again.

*There is a method recommended for rendering
enemies (or friends and acquaintances) motionless:* Seek out the hand of a man recently hanged.
This should be wrapped in a piece of shroud stolen
from a mortuary. It should be tied tightly and each
end securely fastened so that it cannot escape.
Press the hand until all the blood is drained there-
from. Then place the article in an earthen pot or
container. Add thereto some salt, some saltpeter,
and some pepper. Add these ingredients in modera-
tion. Place the container under a cool stairway and
allow it to remain there for fifteen days. When dog
days approach, take the container and place it outside in bright sunlight until the hand is completely
dry. Then prepare a candle. In order to prepare this,
employ grease taken from the hanged man. Collect
wax from altar candles that have never been
burned. Collect a small quantity of sesame from
Lapland. The severed hand, dried, is then converted
into a candlestick by affixing the candles of a de-
filed altar to the tips of the fingers and thumb. Light

116

the candles. Wherever you carry this article, it will prove fatal to some and render most who come in contact with you and it motionless—as if they were dead. Some will become zombie-like and will do whatever you bid them do. If you wish to conquer their souls, you have but to ask, and the souls will be delivered over to you. There must be nothing sexual in the nature of your demands on your subjects. If there is, the hand will shrivel and fall to ashes; your subjects will set upon you, and you will become their slave.

CHAPTER SEVEN

To Gain Wealth and Importance

The legend of the touch of Midas is as well-known as any ever told, and its popularity demonstrates one of the constants of human nature: the desire for wealth and power. It is felt by many that the one means by which an individual can attain fame and fortune is to make a pact with the Devil. This is not entirely true; there are methods described in ancient grimoires that produce the same results but bypass any communication with Satan.

Some of these methods are now put at your disposal; if you want to have luck at games of chance or in general, you need only select the method you wish to employ.

Obtain a virgin piece of parchment, and at the hour of Jove at dawn on the first Thursday of a new moon write on the parchment, "Nom licet ponare in egarbona quia pretium sanguinis." Then cut the head from a snake, preferably one of the poisonous vipers, and fold the corners of the parchment toward each other, enclosing the head of the snake in the center of the parchment. Then, with a silken yellow ribbon, tie the parcel to your left arm. No one must know that you are wearing the article, and no one will know why you are so lucky at games of chance.

The second method also requires the use of a virgin piece of parchment. On the day and hour of the star Mercury at the time when the sun is directly overhead, write the following words on the parchment: "Aba, athi, abotroy, agera, prosha." Place small crosses between each word; these crosses are to be written or drawn in blood from four of your fingers. Do not, however, draw blood from your thumb. The fingers should be those of your left hand and the drawing and writing should be done with your right hand. Sprinkle the parchment and its message with incense taken from a cathedral. Fold the parcel in quarters and carry it in a pocket closest to your heart.

On a virgin piece of parchment, write: "Lo, ma, na, pa, quoa, ra sata, na." Place a silver coin in the center of the parchment and fold the four corners toward each other, then fold again, and then a third time until the parchment is tightly creased over the silver coin. On a Sunday when the sun is bright, prior to midnight, seek out a dirt road that forms a four-corner crossing. In the center of the crossing dig a small hole and bury the parchment and the coin. Stamp the ground firmly with your left foot three times and make nine signs of the cross over the spot. Go away without looking back. The following day, at the same hour, go back to the spot and dig up the parchment and coin. Go away without looking back and without bothering to refill the small hole. Carry the coin and parchment with you always—you will never experience ill fortune.

Gather the following on St. John the Baptist's Day, preferably before dawn: plantane seeds, a goose quill, holy water from a small chapel, and wax gathered from altar candles. Using a mortar and pestle, crush the plantane seeds until they are in powder form. Fill the stem of the goose quill with the powder. Add thereto three drops of holy water taken from a small chapel and seal the ends of the quill with wax gathered from altar candles. Carry this talisman with you wherever you go. Good luck will always be with you when it is on your person.

On the night before the day of St. Peter, search for an herb known as "morsus diaboli" or "St. Joseph's herb" (it is a kind of scabious). When you have found the herb, do not take it into your hands before making on the ground a half-circle that terminates in two crosses. Recite the words: "Aga, adonay, Jehovah." Holding the herb tightly in your left hand, go to the nearest church and place the herb under the altar cloth on the right side of the tabernacle or holy book. Leave it under the cloth for twenty-four hours. After you have retrieved the herb, allow it to dry completely and then crush it in mortar and pestle until it is in the form of a powder. Place the powder in a small sachet, preferably made of silk, and carry the sachet around your neck on a silver chain. If the evening before St. Peter's Day coincides with a full moon, your luck will be even greater.

Before the sun comes up on the first Tuesday of a new moon, search for a four- or five-leafed clover. When you have found it, recite: "Christus, factus est obediens usque ad mortem, mortem autem crucis. Propter quod Deus exaltavit Jeschue." Carry the clover leaf with you everywhere. Good fortune will follow you.

Pick three laurel leaves and offer them up to the good genius Balay. On each leaf write the names of the three archangels, Michael, Gabriel, and Raphael. Carry the three laurel leaves with you always. Whenever you are venturing into a gambling proposition, utter the following: "Balay dat ludenti victorian." You will not lose, whatever the sport.

If you dabble in the lotteries, it is directed that you recite the words of the Creed backwards prior to leaving your residence to buy the tickets. After reciting the Credo, add the words "Lux lucidum lucidentes." Your lottery tickets will bring you your fortune.

The last method is a little more elaborate. First you must find an eel that was washed up on land and died of lack of water. Next, fetch the gall from a bull that has been killed by a pack of mad dogs. Place the gall into the eelskin and sprinkle the gall with additional drops of the bull's blood. Tie the ends of the skin with lengths of rope that served to hang a man. Hide the article for twenty-one days in a heap of manure. Then take it out and dry it thoroughly in a kiln—do this on the eve of St. John's Day. Fashion the dried skin into a wrist-band and write thereon the letters HVTV. The letters should be printed in script, in blood and with a pen never used before. Luck will be yours.

In each of the foregoing methods, it is important to remember that all fortune resulting from the employment of these charms should be shared with the poor. If you fail to do this, ill fortune will plague you always.

When virgin parchment is required, said parchment should be the fairest, cleanest vellum obtainable; it should be made from the hide of a young goat that has never experienced sexual congress with another of its species.

Anyone who stumbles upon a dead bat should cut out the heart of the bat and wear it on his arm, tied with a scarlet thread. (If he wears the eye of that bat he will be rendered invisible.)

Place a large silver ring in the third house of the Moon. Draw in the silver ring (whose table is square) the image of a woman, well-clothed and sitting in a chair with her right hand raised to her head. Seal the picture and sprinkle it with musk, camphor, and calamus aromaticus.

According to Paracelsus, the surest way to obtain good fortune, good health, wisdom, and success is to center one's attention for forty days on an alembic containing a goodly quantity of human semen, preferably another's. At the end of the forty days, there will appear a small human form which will move through the tiny sea of semen. If you feed this embryo with a sprinkling of human blood, preserving it carefully for four weeks at a moderate temperature like the degree of a horse's stomach, a real child will be created. However, the child will be extremely minute and almost the size of an ant. This small being will bring you everlasting good fortune. Another such creature can be made by mixing soil, max, and metal, and not only will the creator have good fortune but he will also possess the power to compel the most beautiful of humans into his embrace, although the creator might turn into a monster of ugliness.

Remove the testicles from a small boy who has been recently hanged. If you want your business to be a thriving success, bury these severed testicles in the basement of your place of business and consecrate them with sale and candle drippings.

To win a lawsuit, take fernseeds and place them in a quill removed from a white goose.

If you have had a kingdom and want to regain it, or if you wish for a foreign empire, wear the alectorius stone. It will bring you that which you desire.

Another talisman to carry on your person is the sardius gem. It carries good luck in its luster.

The red chalcedony will bring good fortune. It should, however, be engraved with the shape of a man holding a scepter.

Always be certain there is money in your pocket, no matter how small the amount; for when one hears the call of the cuckoo and there is money in one's pocket, the cuckoo will follow one in spirit and will bring good luck to the listener wherever he ventures.

Greeting the new moon for the first time with silver coins in the bottom of one's shoe will bring fortune during that period of the new moon.

In order to gain fame and favor, it is advised that one fashion a crown from amaranth (a flower which is one of the symbols of immortality). It will bring fame and wealth to all who wear this crown.

The fat of a killed goose mingled with a handful of fur pulled from a white cat with long hair should be mixed into a potion and smeared on the back of the hand. The substance should be allowed to dry for five days before venturing into a gambling hall or other place of sport.

Treasure hunters are advised to read carefully the following directions in order to obtain success in their ventures: Find first a round agate prior to setting out on your expedition to find treasure. When you have reached the place where supposed treasure is hidden, heat the head of an axe until it is white-hot. Place the axe on the ground so that the white-hot edge is facing upward to the sun. The sun should be directly overhead for the best results. Balance the agate on the hot edge of the axe. If the agate sticks to the edge and does not fall to the ground, then do not look for the treasure, as there is none to be found; however, if the agate falls and rolls away from the axe, you are in luck. There is a treasure in the vicinity. You must repeat this operation, however, three or four times, and the agate should roll in the same direction each time. When this is accomplished, follow the direction in which the agate rolled. Within thirty-one steps the treasure will be found. But if the agate does not roll in the same place each time it is placed on the hot edge of the axe, then you should give up the search and seek treasure another place. Repeat this operation whenever you are in an area where treasure is a likelihood. It will not fail you.

Still another method of uncovering lost treasure (this method is to be employed when searching for treasure in a cave): First make certain that you have a lantern to be used in case you find yourself in pitch blackness. Secure a very large candle, preferably made of beeswax and with some composition of human tallow. Fasten this candle to a structure of hazelwood fashioned in the form of the letter "W." Light the candle when you are in the cavern or cave. If the candle sparks, there is treasure nearby. As you walk with the lighted candle in its hazelwood structure and the candle continues to spark, this means that you are walking closer and closer to the treasure. If the candle merely burns with a constant, even flame then there is no treasure at all in the cave. When you are atop the hiding place of the treasure, the candle will flare and spark and then burn out completely. This is the reason you were advised to carry the lantern. The candle cannot be relighted after it has burned itself out.

In order to keep your home safe from thieves and ill luck: Find first "the Hand of Glory." Rub the portals of the house, all doors and windows and available means of entrance, with this hand's fluids and the gall of a black cat, that of a fat white hen, and the blood of an old screech-owl. These fluids must be gathered in a container made of goatskin and must be gathered on a "dog day."

The following is instruction for doubling one's wealth: First, seize a hair from a mare in heat. This hair must be taken from a place as near to the vulva as possible and must not have the root broken off. As you pull it out, say: "Drigne, dragne." Then go and buy an earthenware pot with a lid on it. It is essential that one not haggle over the price of the pot and lid. Fill the vessel with drinking water until the liquid is three finger-breadths from the rim. Put in the mare's hair, cover the pot, and hide it in some secret place. After nine full days, bring out the pot and you will find in it a sort of little serpent which will rear up quickly. When you see it rear up, say aloud: "I accept the pact." Then take this serpent with your right hand, which is wrapped in kidskin, and shut it in a box made of young pine, which you will have bought without haggling over the price. You will have put into it some wheat bran, which is to feed your serpent, and which must be renewed each morning. Whenever you want silver or gold, you put a little of either in the box, then lie down on your bed near the box and remain motionless for three hours. At the end of this time, open the box and you will find in it twice as much silver or gold as you put into it. When you want to do this again, be careful to place inside the box silver or gold coins which have not already been used for this purpose. Note also that you must not put in more than a hundred coins, and make sure that in your horoscope for the day the Sun is in a favorable aspect with the Moon and free from the harmful influences of Saturn or Mars.

For further good fortune: Would you like to make a Mandragora as powerful as the homunculus so highly praised by Paracelsus? Then find a root of the plant called bryony. Take it out of the ground on a Monday (the day of the Moon) a little time after the vernal equinox. Cut off the ends of the root and bury it at night in some country churchyard in a dead man's grave. For thirty days water it with cow's milk in which three bats have been drowned. When the thirty-first day arrives, take out the root in the middle of the night and dry it in an oven heated with branches of verbena; then wrap it up in a piece of a dead man's winding-sheet and carry it with you everywhere.

Another recipe for mandragora: Take a black hen's egg, and extract as much of the white as would equal in volume a large bean. Replace this white of egg with Sperma Viri (human semen) and seal the egg with a piece of virgin parchment slightly moistened. Then put your egg in a pile of dung on the first day of the March moon which you will find in the table of Epacts. After thirty days of incubation, a tiny monster resembling a human being will come out of the egg. You must keep it hidden in some secret place, feed it with lavender seeds and earthworms. You will have success in everything as long as it lives.

Still another method, but one which is said to lose its beneficial effect after twenty years, consists in bleeding a black chicken during the night at a cross-roads where four paths meet. As you cut its throat, say: "Berit, do my work for twenty years," and bury the chicken very deep so that dogs and other wild animals will not be attracted to the place. The spirit thus invoked will follow you everywhere and will bring you success.

Or do your modest wishes extend merely to the acquisition of enough money to last you until the end of the year? In that case, make some pancakes with eggs, milk, and flour while, in the church nearest your house, the first mass of Candlemas is being said (on the day of the Purification of the Holy Virgin), and try to make a dozen pancakes before the mass is ended.

Any mandragora or homunculus created can be gotten rid of. The black book says that the possession of these creations is not without danger. When you want to get rid of them, you must write on a piece of virgin parchment the name and the sign of the spirit Clamey, put the writing in a box, and put in a handful of flour with which a priest has said his first mass. The pacts will then be broken.

CHAPTER EIGHT

The Use of Talismans

Amulets are passive charms, designed to protect the wearer from certain difficulties, such as an amulet to ward off the effects of the evil eye. The talisman is a more active form of magic; it may provide a very specific protection, or it may obtain certain results. Marianne Verneuil, in her *Dictionnaire Pratique des Sciences Occultes*, explains, "The amulet utilizes natural objects . . . and operates through its own inherent virtue, whilst the talisman is the product of intellectual speculation and magical fabrication . . . directed toward a specific end."

Talismans have been made of many substances and in many forms. The fundamental talismans are seven, corresponding to the days of the week, and the formulas for producing them are strictly outlined.

The Talisman of Saturn: This talisman acts especially as a preservative against apoplexy, dropsy, paralysis, phthisis, consumption, cancer, and decaying of the bones, especially against death as a result of these and as a protection against being buried alive or violent death through such means as poison, ambush, or secret plotting. It protects women as well from the mortal dangers of childbirth. And should the leader of an army hide the Talisman of Saturn in some location which is about to fall into the hands of the enemy, that enemy will prove unable to cross the region of the hidden talisman and will retreat.

For the making of the talisman, one must obtain a plaque of the purest lead, which is cut in the form of a circle about the size of a religious medal, both faces polished smoothly.

On one side of this medal a diamond-pointed burin or graver is employed to engrave the image of a scythe, which is enclosed in a star with five points, or a pentagram. On the opposite side must be engraved a six-pointed star enclosing the head of a bull, and about the star letters composing the name Rempha (according to the alphabet of the Magi), which is the planetary genius of Saturn.

The one who is to wear the talisman must do this engraving himself, with no witnesses to the deed and without informing any other of his intention. He must choose for the task a Saturday, which is the day of Saturn, when the evolution of the Moon is passing through the first ten degrees of Taurus or Capricorn, in a favorable aspect with Saturn.

To determine whether or not there is a favorable aspect between Saturn and the Moon, one must cast one's own horoscope on the nearest Saturday containing the lunar evolution mentioned. If Saturn is trine or sextile with the Moon, that is in a favorable aspect, and that day will be good for working on this talisman. But if the Moon and Saturn are in square or in opposition, another Saturday must be tried until a favorable aspect is found. When a favorable day is found, one must perform the work at the favorable hours, or those which are governed by Saturn. These would be from midday to one o'clock, from seven to eight in the evening, from two until three A.M. after that midnight (which is to say, the following day, as the day for this purpose is reckoned from one midday to the next), and from nine until ten A.M. If the work is not completed during one of these periods, it must be set aside and taken up again in the next hourly period.

When the making of the talisman is done, it must be consecrated. For this purpose the talisman is exposed to fumes from a preparation of alum, asafoetida, scammony, and sulphur, burned with cyprus, ash, and black hellebore; these are lighted in an earthenware dish which has never been used for any other purpose. When the ceremony is complete, this must be ground to dust and buried secretly in a rarely visited spot. Having been thus consecrated, the talisman is placed in a sachet of black silk and worn on the breast by means of black silk bands interwoven and tied in the form of a cross.

The Talisman of Jupiter: This talisman has as its special properties the driving away of all cares, and favor to honest works and better social standing. It brings to the wearer the good will and sympathy of others. In addition, it affords protection against unexpected accidents and those violent deaths which may be presaged by Saturn in the natal horoscope. The wearer is also protected from death which might result from malignant tumors, liver diseases, or inflammation of the lungs.

To make a Talisman of Jupiter, one requires a plaque of purest tin, cut into a circle as above and polished smoothly. Using a diamond-pointed burin, the intended wearer inscribes on one face the image of a crown with four points, this placed at the center of a pentagram. On the opposite side he draws the image of an eagle's head within a six-pointed star, which is surrounded by letters composing the name Pi-Zeus according to the alphabet of the Magi, this being the planetary genius of Jupiter.

For the work, which one must do without witnesses and informing no one of one's intention, a Thursday must be chosen when the evolution of the Moon is passing through the first ten degrees of Libra and is in a favorable aspect, sextile or trine, with Saturn and Jupiter.

To determine whether this aspect is favorable, the horoscope must be drawn up on the first Thursday containing the mentioned lunar evolution. If the aspect is unfavorable, successive Thursdays must be tried until a good one is found. The favorable hours are from midday to one o'clock, from seven until eight in the evening, from two until three A.M., and from nine until ten of the following morning.

For the consecration, frankincense, ambergris, balsam, cardamon, saffron, and mace are burned with oak, poplar, fig, and pomegranate branches in an earthenware vessel which is afterward disposed of as above. The sachet in this instance is to be made of sky-blue silk.

The Talisman of Mars: This talisman especially protects its wearer against the attack of dangerous enemies. It protects also against death in battle or as a result of argument, from epidemic, malignant ulcers, or St. Anthony's fire. If the natal horoscope has presaged violent death by torture, the Talisman of Mars will offset this danger. If it is hidden within a citadel by the commanding officer, the place will be saved from attack.

For the making of this talisman, there is needed a plaque as described above, but of very pure iron. Following the prescriptions previously advanced, the individual engraves on one side a pentagram enclosing an image of swords crossed. On the opposite side is engraved the six-pointed star, within which is a lion's head, and about which are the letters according to the alphabet of the Magi which spell Ertosi, the planetary genius of Mars.

This work must be done on a Tuesday while the evolution of the Moon passes through the first ten degrees of the Ram or Saggitarius and is found in favorable aspect with Mars and Saturn. To determine the condition, the horoscope is set up on the nearest Tuesday containing the lunar evolution with Saturn and Mars in favorable aspect as described. The favorable hours are from midday to one o'clock, from seven until eight in the evening, from two until three in the morning, and from nine until ten the following morning.

The consecration will require fumes from desiccated absinthe and rue, with the dish disposed of as before. The sachet for this talisman will be of red silk.

The Talisman of the Sun: The wearers of this talisman will enjoy the good will and favorable disposition of others in high positions. Also, they will be protected from death by epidemic or conflagration.

Nor need they have fears of death from heart disease or syncope.

The directions above are to be followed in the making of this talisman, which will be prepared from a plaque of pure gold. The engraving on the first side will be of a circle within the pentagram. On the second side will be a human head within the six-pointed star, the whole surrounded by the letters according to the alphabet of the Magi which compose the name Pi-Rhe, the planetary genius of the Sun.

This work must be done on a Sunday when the evolution of the Moon is passing through the first ten degrees of the Lion and is in favorable aspect with Saturn and the Sun. To determine the favorability the horoscope is drawn up on the nearest Sunday containing the lunar evolution with a favorable aspect of the Moon with the Sun and Saturn. The favorable hours of work are as above. The consecration, carried out as above, requires cinnamon, frankincense, saffron, and red sandalwood, burned with laurel and dried heliotrope stalks in an earthenware dish. A sachet of pale yellow silk is advised.

The Talisman of Venus: Those desiring harmony and affection between man and wife will wear this talisman, as it especially favors such matters. Among its other properties, if one dips the talisman into a liquid and then persuades an enemy, however bitter, to drink thereof, his hatred will be transformed into affection and loving devotion. Moreover, it protects against violent death by poisoning. It protects women especially from cancer. If the natal horoscope presages danger according to the influence of Mars, this talisman will offset such tendency.

In making the talisman, following the directions above, a plaque of purest copper is needed. The engraving of the first side will be the pentacle containing the letter G (as it occurs in the alphabet of the Magi). On the second side is engraved a dove within a six-pointed star, about which are the letters of the alphabet of the Magi which compose the name Suroth, the planetary genius of Venus.

For the work, a Friday must be chosen when the evolution of the Moon is passing through the first ten degrees of Taurus or the Virgin and is found in favorable aspect with Saturn and Venus. To determine if this aspect is favorable the horoscope is drawn up on the nearest Friday containing the lunar evolution with the Moon in favorable aspect with Saturn and Venus. The hours suitable for work are as above.

The consecration of this talisman requires its exposure to the fumes of violets and roses burned with olive wood according to the above directions. The sachet for this talisman will be of either green or pink silk.

The Talisman of Mercury: This talisman affords special protection to every kind of commerce and industry. It will attract clients and prosperity if buried in the ground beneath a place of business. It protects the wearer against madness and epilepsy, and from death by murder or poison. It prevents treason, and if placed under the pillow during sleep it will produce dreams of a prophetic nature.

The directions for making the talisman are as above, except that the plaque must be composed of an alloy of tin, silver, and mercury.

On the first side one engraves a pentagram, in which is a winged caduceus with two serpents entwined about it. On the other side is engraved the six-pointed star, within which is a dog's head, and about which are the letters (according to the alphabet of the Magi) which compose the name Pi-Hermes, the planetary genius of Mercury.

Wednesday is the day consecrated to Mercury, and this day must be chosen for the work, when the evolution of the Moon is passing through the first ten degrees of Gemini or Scorpio and is in favorable aspect with Saturn and Mercury. To determine whether the aspect is favorable, the horoscope is set up on the nearest Wednesday containing the lunar evolution with a favorable aspect of the Moon with Saturn and Mercury.

The hours are as above. The consecration requires fumes of benzoin, mace, and storax burned with the dried stalks of lilies, narcissus, marjoram, and fumitory (a plant of the genus *Fumaria*). A sachet of purple silk is needed for this talisman.

The Talisman of the Moon: This is the talisman which protects those traveling or dwelling in foreign lands. In addition it protects the wearer from death by shipwreck, and from madness, apoplexy, epilepsy, and dropsy. If the Saturnine aspects of the horoscope presage violent death, this talisman will keep such perils at bay.

The directions for making this talisman are the same as for those preceding, except that the plaque must be of very pure silver. On one side is engraved the image of a crescent within the pentagram. On the opposite side is the six-pointed star enclosing a goblet and surrounded by the letters of the alphabet of the Magi which compose the name Pi-Ioh. This work must be done on a Monday, the day which is consecrated to the Moon, and when the lunar evolution is passing through the first ten degrees of the Virgin or of Capricorn and is found in favorable aspect with Saturn. The horoscope must be set up on the nearest Monday containing the lunar evolution as described, and at the hours noted above.

For the consecration of this talisman, one exposes it to the fumes of white sandalwood, camphor, aloes, amber, and pounded cucumber seeds, burned with dried stalks of artemisia (a strongly scented herb), selenotrope, and ranunculus. The talisman is placed in a sachet of white silk.

These are the traditional talismans. If one needs further aid with the question of horoscopes, one should consult a work on this specific subject, which is too complex to be fully explained in this volume.

CHAPTER NINE

Diverse Charms (Amulets and Spells and Superstitions)

The virtues of the precious stones:
Amethyst: This stone, transparent and of a purple hue, emits rosy sparkles. The Indian variety is the most precious. When made into drinking cups or bound to the navel, it will assuredly prevent a person from becoming drunk. The amethyst gives the wearer the gift of tongues and the ability to prophesy. If the stone is worn by a woman, it will ensure her husband's love. Amethysts originated in Russia; however, fine stones are found in the Rio Grande du Sul district of Brazil and in Northern Uruguay. The stone can also be found in India, Ceylon, and Madagascar. It occurs in the cavities of ancient volcanic rocks, especially basalt. The amethyst is considered to be the royal stone, and should be worn by all born in the month of February. According to the Bible, the amethyst is the symbol of perfection.

Aquamarine (a variety of beryl): This stone belongs to the same family as the emerald. It comes from Ceylon, Brazil, Maine and North Carolina in the United States, and Russia. It is sea-green to blue in color, and its wearer will be endowed with courage and strength. It is a cure for laziness and quickens the intellect. It should be worn by all those born during the month of March. Beryl, it should be noted, has the power to aid happiness in marriage. Further, the sea-green beryl, when set in gold and engraved with the figure of a frog, will grant the wearer the affection of all those who touch it or are touched by it. If the stone is dipped into water, all who drink the water will grant eternal friendship to the wearer of the beryl.

Crystal: If a string of crystal stones is worn around the neck, it will increase the supply of milk in a nursing mother. Donning crystal before retiring will induce deep sleep and grant the wearer very pleasant dreams. It is also capable of producing visions. All dreams will be pleasant ones.

Diamond: It is believed that the wearer of diamonds will have the capacity to ward off witches, madness, and terrors of the night. Also, the diamond itself possesses many virtues. To him who wears it, it will bring victory; and if it is bound to the wearer's left arm, however many his enemies, he will emerge from the fray successfully and victory will be his. The diamond repels panics, pestilence, and enchantments. It is a cure for sleepwalking and insanity. The Arabian diamond attracts metal more powerfully than any magnet. It cannot be melted by fire and no blow will overcome it. If the diamond is tied to a strong magnet, it will be milked dry of its powers.

Emerald: The emerald is one of the most valuable objects in the world today. The depths of the emerald carry the key to happiness in love and domestic bliss. For a woman the stone brings safety in childbearing. It is the symbol of kindness. The emerald is mined in Upper Egypt, North Carolina in the United States, Australia, Siberia, and Colombia, South America. It is the birthstone of those born in May. It is a preservative of chastity.

Garnet: The garnet preserves health and promotes happiness for its wearer. If the wearer be a lover, however, it can cause discord. If a lion is engraved on the surface of the stone it preserves good health and protects travelers. It repels epidemics. The garnet should be worn by those born in January. It is a lucky talisman. It represents constancy, true friendship, and fidelity, but is not to be worn by lovers at any time. Its power rests with the family and friends. The popularity of the garnet reached its peak during the Victorian era, although it is said that the only light in the Ark of Noah was produced by enormous red garnets mounted in the overhead beams. The rarest garnets are found in the Ural Mountains.

Moonstone: The wearer of the moonstone will have good will and lasting friendships. It is the symbol of happiness. Because of its radiance, it is believed to be capable of banishing fears and nightmares. It should be worn by those born in the month of June, but it is an extremely rare stone.

Onyx: This black stone should be worn only by men. It is a symbol of virility, and if worn with a diamond in its center it signifies that the man is bisexual in nature. The ring should never be worn on the smallest finger of either hand, or it will only bring scorn upon the wearer. If it is engraved with the head of a camel, it will give the wearer terrifying dreams. Although a strong stone, it is a dire one.

Opal: This gem is worn to dispel sadness. If you are disheartened for any reason, wear an opal on your person—it will lighten the spirits and make the wearer of good cheer. It is the symbol of hope. Upon the marriage of each of Queen Victoria's daughters, gifts of opals were bestowed upon them. The "fire" opals are found in Mexico; the "harlequin" opals are found chiefly in Czechoslovakia; "black" opals come from Australia, as do the "white" or "milk" opals. Opals should be worn by those born in October.

Pearl: This is the stone that will comfort the heart. It will cause its wearer to remain chaste despite all trials and tribulations. The best and finest pearls are found in the Persian Gulf, the South Seas, and the coastal waters of Australia. It is another good luck stone for all those born in the month of June.

Ruby: This is the gem of the sun. It is a symbol of regal position. It is one of the most precious gems in the world. It is the sign of freedom, charity, dignity, and divine power. The finest stones come from the Far East; the true pigeon's-blood rubies are mined in Mogok, in Upper Burma. Some rubies have been found in North Carolina. The Ruby brings good fortune to those born in the month of July.

Sapphire: The sapphire, a blue stone, brings cheer to the wearer and grants a man power and vigor of body. It is considered to be an amulet against gruesome happenings and fears. If a ram is engraved on the face of the sapphire it will cure inflammations of the eyes, preserve chastity, and promote good fortune. It is the prized oriental gem, and represents truth, sincerity, and faithfulness. It was a belief of the Persians that the earth rested on a sapphire whose reflection gave color to the sky. The finest sapphires come from the Cashmere district of India, and also from Ceylon, Upper Burma, and Siam. There are slightly inferior gems found in North Carolina, in Montana, in the Rhine region in Germany, and some in France. It is the birthstone for those born during September.

Sardonyx: This beautiful red stone, if set in silver, platinum, or brazen gold and engraved with the head of an eagle, will bring the wearer good luck.

Topaz: A golden yellow gem which, if engraved with a falcon, will preserve chastity and gain sympathy for the wearer. If it is worn on the left hand it will cause melancholy to vanish.

Turquoise: This stone makes a good amulet against accidents when on horseback. It will also prevent its wearer from becoming tired. It helps ward off danger and clears one's path of pitfalls.

The virtues of miscellaneous stones, herbs, and minerals:

If one carries a lodestone in his left hand, he will be able to walk through a field of vipers without injury.

If one wishes to render the evil eye harmless, one must simply wear a fleur-de-lis of gold, silver, or enamel.

Calundronius is considered to be the magic stone which destroys enchantments and gives its owner an advantage over all enemies and obstacles.

The agate or achates will act as a repellent against the bite of the scorpion or any poisonous snake. It drives contagion from the air and stops thunder and lightning if held up to the skies. It is also capable of ending solitude, promoting eloquence, and securing the favors of persons of royal background. All enemies shrink in fear when they see this stone on the third finger of a man's left hand.

Malachite is a preserver of the cradle. It protects infants from sickness and other bodily ills.

Carbuncle, which is considered fifth among the stones in value, gives out a native light without reflection. It is ruled by the sun and it purifies the air, represses luxury, and preserves the health of the wearer. It also has the power of reconciling enemies.

Balasius is a stone of a purple or rose color and is called by some "the placidus" or "the pleasant." Its virtue lies in its ability to overcome vanity—it can heal arguments among friends and it befriends humans if they are of good health. If the four corners of any house and garden are touched with the balasius, the property will be safe from lightning, tempests, and worms.

Lignite, if hung around the neck, will protect the wearer from witchcraft in any form. It is a beautiful stonelike glass gem easily available.

Lippares or liparia is a stone worn by those who wish to capture wild beasts, but the beast who looks upon the stone can never have been attacked by either man or dog.

Draconite, dentrite, draconius, or obsianus is the name of a shiny black stone shaped like a pyramid. It makes its wearer invincible. It is only to be gotten from the head of a slain dragon, and its power will wane if the stone is not removed from the dragon's head while the dragon is still panting with life.

Chalcedony dispels phantoms, removes illusions and evil spirits. It gives the body power, and those who wear this stone will make fortunes in law. It should, for best results, be perforated and suspended by ass's hairs. If the gem is of the black variety it will give one a beautiful singing voice and will prevent hoarseness.

Chelidonius is a stone found in the entrails of the swallow. It is a good talisman against melancholy and periodical disorders.

Chrysolite prevents fever and madness. If it is put into a gold setting it will act as a preservative against nocturnal terrors.

Chrisoletus, if bound with gold and carried in the left hand, will ward off hags and witches and will protect one from melancholia.

Chrysoprase is a good stone for curing weakness of the eyes and for procuring joyful news. Its color is green and gold.

Andordama resembles a diamond somewhat and is said to be found in the sands of the Red Sea. It is the magnet for attracting virtuous individuals to the wearer and restrains one from anger and insanity.

The wearer of antiphates will be defended against all forms of witchcraft. It is a stone similar to the onyx.

Salagrama is a stone black in color and is native to India. If it is imprisoned in a clean cloth and washed every day in warm water and perfumed with musk it will expell all sin from the wearer.

Due to the color of agapis, it is a promoter of love and charity. It is also used to cure poisonous viper bites.

Ash trees, if burned at Christmas time, will bring prosperity to the family. Ash wards off venomous animals, and if it is used in the construction of a vehicle the vehicle will never suffer an accident or cause injury to its passengers. If the handles of tools and implements are made of ash, the user will never suffer harm or injury.

If the red buds of the ash tree are eaten on St. John's Eve, the eater thereof will be invulnerable to the influence of witches.

If, when searching out the elder tree, you note a branch that forms a crutch, cut out the knot betwixt the two branches forming the crutch and hang it around the neck of a sick person. He will be made well.

Before pruning an elder tree, the gardener should ask permission of the tree, as it has a great influence on witchcraft. The gardener must ask, "Elder, elder, may I cut thy branches?" If the tree gives no answer it is safe to continue with the work, but the gardener should spit three times in three different directions before commencing the pruning.

Laurel branches will give men protection from the elements, from evil spirits, and from lightning.

In order to drive away an evil spirit, make yourself a switch of elder or mountain ash.

To ward off witches from the house, make a ball of green grass and suspend it from the front window of the house.

Another method of warding off evil spirits or witches is to bury a knife under the front doorstep of the house. Witches cannot pass over cold steel.

For protection against werewolves, wear sprigs or twigs of the yew tree, rye, mistletoe, or ash.

Pieces from the wild angelica plant are the best protective measure against evil spells.

Jacinth or hyacinth acts as a protector against plague and lightning and promotes wealth and good fortune.

Jasper gives eloquence and strengthens the intellect.

For good luck, throw rose petals into an open fire.

In case of excessive bleeding, hang red coral around the neck of the victim. It will also protect against infection, evil spells, goblins, and sorceresses. If the coral is ground into powder and sprinkled on the roof of the house, it will protect the house and all its occupants from disaster from the elements.

Secure three nails or screws from a coffin recently dug up from a churchyard and fashion them into a ring. This will act as a charm against insanity and convulsions.

The most effective ore for warding off evil is iron.

If you have been robbed, gather sunflower and laurel leaves picked when the sun is passing through the sign of Leo. Place these, together with a wolf's tooth, under your pillow, and your dream will show the face of the person who robbed you.

To keep witches and evil spirits away, lay a broom beneath your pillow.

From an Egyptian magic tablet, this incantation is against noxious animals:
    Come to me, O Lord of Gods!
    Drive far from me
    The lions coming from the earth,
    The Crocodiles issuing from the river,
    The mouth of all biting reptiles coming out of
        their holes!

Stop, Crocodile Mako, son of Set!
Do not wave thy tail:
Do not work thy two arms:
Do not open thy mouth.
May water become as a burning fire before thee!
The spear of the seventy-seven gods is on thine
eyes:
The arm of the seventy-seven gods is on thine
eye:
Thou who wast fastened with metal claws
To the bark of Ra,
Stop, crocodile Mako, son of Set!

This Egyptian spell is to keep beetles away from corpses:
Depart from me,
O thou hast lips which gnaw;
For I am Khnemu
The Lord of Peshennu,
And I bring words of the gods to Ra,
And I report my message to the lord thereof.

A Babylonian exorcism:
May the wicked demon depart.
May the demons seize one another.
The propitious demon,
The propitious giant,
May they penetrate his body.
Spirit of the Heavens, conjure it!
Spirit of the earth, conjure it!

A Babylonian charm for bewitchment:
Hearken to my prayer. Free me from my bewitch-
ment.
Loosen my sin.
Let there be turned aside whatever evil may come
To cut off my life.

*This is a Chaldean charm to prevent demons from
entering a house:*
Talisman, talisman,
Boundary that cannot be taken away,
Boundary that the gods cannot pass,
Barrier immovable,
Which is opposed to malevolence!
Whether it be a wicked Utuq,
A wicked Alal,
A wicked Gigim,
A wicked god,
A wicked Maskim,
A phantom,
A specter,
A vampire,
An incubus,
A succubus,
A nightmare,
May the barrier of the god Ea stop him!

*This Graeco-Egyptian spell is regarded as especially
binding upon the spirits invoked:*
I call upon thee that didst create the earth and
bones,
And all flesh and all spirit,
That didst establish the sea
And that shakest the heavens,
That didst divide the light from the darkness,
The great regulative mind,
That disposeth everything,
Eye of the world,
Spirit of spirits,
God of gods,
The Lord of Spirits,
Lord of Spirits,
The immovable Aeon,

Iaoouei,
Hear my voice.
I call upon thee
The ruler of the Gods,
High thundering Zeus,
Zeus, king,
Adonnai, lord
Iaoouee.
I am he that invokes thee, the great god,
Zaalaer, Iphphou,
Do thou not disregard the Hebrew appellation,
Ablanthanalb, Abrasiloa.
For I am Silthakhookh, Lailam, Blasaloth,
Iao, Ieo, Nebouth, Sabiothar,
Both, Arbathiao, Iaoth, Saboath,
Patoure, Zagoure, Baroukh,
Adonai, Eloai, Iabraam,
Barbarauo, Nau, Siph.

A Greek magical invocation to Great Bear:
   I invoke you, holy ones, mighty, majestic, glorious
      luminaries,
   Holy and earth-born, mighty arch-demons:
   Dwelling in Chaos, Erebus, and the unfathomable
      abyss.
   Guardians of secrets,
   Captains of the Hosts of Hell;
   Omnipotent, holy, invincible,
   Perform my commands.

*A Chinese spell to be inscribed on a sword, to make
it very powerful:*
   I wield the large sword of Heaven
   To cut down specters in five shapes;
   One stroke of this divine blade
   Disperses a myriad of these beings.

A Persian charm against evil: Get thee a feather of the wide-feathered bird Varenjana, O Spitama Zarathustra. With that feather thou shalt rub thy body; with that feather thou shalt curse back thine enemy. He who hath a bone of the mighty bird or a feather of the mighty bird gaineth divine favor. No one, however magnificent, smiteth him or turneth him to flight.

This is a Roman charm to be put on the opponent's horses when betting: "I summon you demon and hand over to you these horses to keep them and bind them so that they cannot move."

A Hindu spell from Atharva Veda, for becoming immortal:
  Immortality be upon this one! He is a sharer
  Of the sun's everlasting life.
  Indra and Agni have blessed him
  And have taken him into immortality.
  Bhaga and Soma are with him,
  Carrying him high, to prolong his days.

  There will now be no danger of death.
  This world will keep you, forever, rise up!
  The Sun, the Wind, the Rain, are all with thee!

  Thy body shall be strong and unaffected
  By any disease.
  Life will be thine, I promise it;
  Enter this ascending, never-perishing, age-old
    chariot.

  Savitar, the Saver, will guard thee, taking into
    converse
  The great Vayu, of the living, Indra;

And strength and breath shall be with thee;
The spirit of life will ever remain.
No illness shall touch thee;
All powers are on thy side.

A Sanskrit spell for acquiring a husband: "I seek a husband. Sitting here, my hair flowing loose, I am like one positioned before a giant procession, searching for a husband for this woman without a spouse.

"O Aryaman! This woman cannot longer attend the marriages of other women. Now, having performed this rite, other women will come to her wedding feast!

"The creator hold up the Earth, the planets, the Heavens.

"O Creator, produce for me a suitor, a husband!"

A Sanskrit spell for virility: "Thou art the plant which Varuna had dug up for him by Gandharva, thou potent and lusty herb, which we have uprooted.

"Ushas, Surya, Pragapati, all are with me; all will give me the potent force I seek! O Indra, give this material power; it has heat like that of the fire. Like the he-antelope, O Herb, thou hast all the force there is, as the brother of the great Soma."